ULTIMATE AUDITION BOOK
VOLUME II

222 Monologues
2 Minutes and Under
from Literature

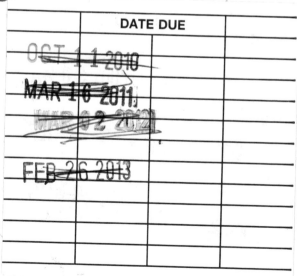

Smith and Kraus Monologue Books

If you require prepublication information about upcoming Smith and Kraus books,
you may receive our semiannual catalogue, free of charge, by sending your name
and address to Smith and Kraus catalogue, PO Box 127, Lyme, NH 03768. Or call us
at (800) 895-4331, fax (603) 922-3348 or find us on the web www.smithkraus.com.

THE ULTIMATE AUDITION BOOK VOLUME II

222 Monologues
2 Minutes and Under from Literature

EDITED BY JOHN CAPECCI,
LAURIE WALKER, AND IRENE ZIEGLER

MONOLOGUE AUDITION SERIES

A Smith and Kraus Book

7-04 19.95

A Smith and Kraus Book
Published by Smith and Kraus, Inc.
177 Lyme Road, Hanover, NH 03755
www.smithkraus.com

Copyright ©2002 by Smith and Kraus
All rights reserved
Manufactured in the United States of America

Cover and Text Design by Julia Gignoux, Freedom Hill Design

First Edition: Feb 2002
10 9 8 7 6 5 4 3 2

The Library of Congress Cataloging-In-Publication Data
The ultimate audition book: two hundred monologues, two minutes and under from literature / edited by John Capecci, Laurie Walker, and Irene Ziegler. —1st ed.
p. cm. —(Monologue audition series)
Includes bibliographical references.
ISBN 1-57525-270-8 vol.2
1. Monologues. 2. Acting—Auditions. 3. Drama. I. Beard, Jocelyn. II. Series.
PN2080.U48   1997
808.82'45—dc21   97-10471
                        CIP

Contents

MEN'S MONOLOGUES

MALE OR FEMALE MONOLOGUES

INTRODUCTION

What makes a monologue exciting to perform, watch, or learn from? The monologues in *The Ultimate Audition Book II,* culled from accomplished writing, all have the intensity and immediacy that make a performer want to dig in, an audience want to listen. They are charged with a pulsing voice. They beg to breathe.

The Ultimate Audition Book II is a collection of 222 monologues drawn from literary works not traditionally considered for performance. Because they clock in at two minutes or under, they can be combined in hundreds of ways to suit your audition, classroom, or workshop needs. Here are over a hundred monologues for women, over a hundred for men, and selections from both contemporary and classic texts.

Within this collection you are sure to find monologues new to you. As performance specialists, we know that lifting literary characters off the shelf and giving them life through performance is exciting. Unless you're an avid reader, though, the search for performable literature can be daunting. You may be a working actor looking for fresh audition material, or a student performer honing your skills. Perhaps you're a teacher or a coach, or you may be a reader—a category we hope cuts across all others. Readers know that to craft compelling characters is not the province of playwrights alone. The monologues in *The Ultimate Audition Book II* come primarily from prose works: novels, novellas, memoirs, short stories, essays, and narrative poetry. Whoever you are, and whatever your interest in monologues, we hope *The Ultimate Audition Book II* will serve as both a useful sourcebook, and an inspiration for mining literature other than plays for rich, dramatic gems.

The Selection Process. What is a monologue? In *The Ultimate Audition Book II,* a monologue is a short, self-contained excerpt that features a central speaker and contains some change in thought, emotion, or action. The monologues in this book were chosen to highlight the following:

Established authors, lesser-known works. We have attempted to find works not frequently included in other collections. (But there are a few favorites we just couldn't pass up.) We've also attempted to excerpt the monologues with a minimum of editing. Where editing was necessary, omissions are indicated by parenthetical ellipses (…). All other ellipses were part of the original text.

Varied characters. While we believe it is important to include a diversity of writers, it seems most crucial to offer you a wide variety of characters in terms of *sex, age, tone, time period, and voice*.

You'll find the monologues arranged and indexed according to these characteristics, with cross-referencing to help identify those most suited to your needs.

> **Age** is indicated exactly only when specified by the author. More often, we've indicated an age range. In some instances, we've used a plus sign (+) to show the character could be older than indicated, as in 60+. In a few instances, the author has made no indication as to the adult speaker's age. These monologues are included as 20+.

> **Tone** refers to whether a monologue falls into one of the following general categories: comic, seriocomic, dramatic.

> **Time Period** refers to the time period in which the character is speaking, not when the monologue was written.

> **Voice** refers to any markers of class, geography, ethnicity, nationality, sexual identity, or narrative style that may help a performer gain entry into an individual monologue.

Varied styles. Works written as early as 700 A.D. and as recently as 2000 appear in *The Ultimate Audition Book II*, offering a range of styles and mirroring the requirements of the standard professional audition. Recognizing that performers who turn to literary works often favor first-person monologues, *The Ultimate Audition Book II* also includes second- and third-person works for the opportunities those points of view offer.

Varied Contexts: Whether stepping out of a bathtub or stepping into a fight, the speaker is specifically located, both physically and psychologically. If it is identified in the original work, each monologue is accompanied by a brief description of the speaker's world to help orient your approach.

This book was born of many loves: the love of language and literature, of fine performance, art, and story. Above all else, it was born of an insatiable fascination with people, and with the very varied things they say and do.

This is the province of the performer. As a performer, you introduce us, your audience, to people we might otherwise never meet, enrich our experience of what it is to be human. You show and you tell.

So dig in, have at it! Captivate and be captivated. Let a word within spur you to higher heights, wider reading. Charles Baxter says "We understand our lives, or try to, by the stories we tell."

Begin.
And break a leg.

Women's Monologues

8 Ball Chicks: A Year in the Violent World of Girl by Gini Sikes

Novel
F, 16
New York, contemporary
Dramatic

Tiny is a member of a girl gang, the Nasty Fly Ladies, in New York's Lower East Side. Tiny is five feet tall, in droopy pants and an oversized windbreaker.

• • •

See, we smaller girls, we go for your weak spot. (...) Your face. Your throat. Your eyes, so we can blind you. I don't care if you have more weight on me. I'll still try to kill you because, you know, I have a bad temper—(...)

Let me break it down for you: round here it's all about respect. Because people will disrespect you. Call you a sucker. And if you don't punch them in the mouth and say, "No, I'm not a sucker!" they gonna keep picking on you. Nowadays the fists don't work no more. You gotta have a knife or a hammer. Or a gun. 'Cause my homegirl got shot in the stomach. Lost her kidney. (...)

See, we formed NFL to protect ourselves. (. . .) Nobody's out there we can trust but ourselves. And we defend each other. Ain't nobody else gonna do it for us. (...)

If I see you coming down the street and I think you have money, I'll rob you. (...) Out here we only go for Chinese or white people. They got money. I won't rob her—(she pointed to an elderly woman outside)—because she's old.(...) But I'll rob her—as fast as I'll rob you. It don't matter. We do it for fun. Sometimes to get high or to buy something to drink. If we go out dancing, we catch a herb first. We can have money in our pockets and we'll still do it. (...)

'Cause we have nothing to live for, nothing to lose.

"An Angel" from *Good Bones and Simple Murders* by Margaret Atwood

Short story
F, 20+
Contemporary
Dramatic

A contemplation upon the angel of suicide.

• • •

I know what the angel of suicide looks like. I have seen her several times. She's around.

She's nothing like the pictures of angels you run across here and there, the ones in classical paintings, with their curls and beautiful eyelashes, or the ones on Christmas cards, all cute or white. (...)

Not so the angel of suicide, who is dense, heavy with antimatter, a dark star. But despite the differences, she does have something in common with those others. All angels are messengers, and so is she; which isn't to say that all messages are good. (...)

Angels come in two kinds: the others, and those who fell. The angel of suicide is one of those who fell, down through the atmosphere to the earth's surface. Or did she jump? With her you have to ask. (...)

They said, the pack of them, I will not serve. The angel of suicide is one of those: a rebellious waitress. Rebellion, that's what she has to offer, to you, when you see her beckoning to you from outside the window, fifty stories up, or the edge of the bridge, or holding something out to you, some emblem of release, soft chemical, quick metal.

Wings, of course. You wouldn't believe a thing she said if it weren't for the wings.

As I Lay Dying by **William Faulkner**

Novel
F, 50+
Mississippi, 1930s
Dramatic

*Addie Bundren is dying. She is propped up in bed, looking
out of the window as one of her hapless sons builds her
coffin.*

• • •

In the afternoon when school was out and the last one had left
with his little dirty snuffling nose, instead of going home I would go
down the hill to the spring where I could be quiet and hate them. It
would be quiet there then, with the water bubbling up and away
and the sun slanting quiet in the trees and the quiet smelling of
damp and rotting leaves and new earth; especially in the early
spring, for it was worst then.

I could just remember how my father used to say that the reason for
living was to get ready to stay dead a long time. And when I would
have to look at them day after day, each with his and her secret and
selfish thought, and blood strange to each other blood and strange
to mine, and think that this seemed to be the only way I could get
ready to stay dead, I would hate my father for having ever planted
me. I would look forward to the times when they faulted, so I could
whip them. When the switch fell I could feel it upon my flesh:
When it welted and ridged it was my blood that ran, and I would
think with each blow of the switch: Now you are aware of me! Now
I am something in your secret and selfish life, who have marked
your blood with my own for ever and ever.

"At Fifty" by Jenny Diski

Essay
F, 50
Contemporary
Dramatic

*A British woman, at age 50, remembers herself as a child
who is trying to imagine what turning 50 might be like.*

• • •

I'm nine years old, in bed, in the dark. The detail in the room is perfectly clear. I am lying on my back. I have a greeny-gold quilted
eiderdown covering me. I have just calculated that I will be 50 years
old in 1997. "Fifty" and "1997" don't mean a thing to me, aside
from being an answer to an arithmetic question I set myself. I try it
differently. "I will be 50 in 1997." 1997 doesn't matter. "I will be
50." The statement is absurd. I am nine. "I will be ten" makes
sense. "I will be 13" has a dreamlike maturity about it. "I will be
50" is simply a paraphrase for another senseless statement I make
to myself at night: "I will be dead one day." "One day I won't be." I
have a great determination to feel the sentence as a reality. But it
always escapes me. "I will be dead" comes with a picture of a dead
body on a bed. But it's mine, a nine-year-old body. When I make it
old, it becomes someone else. I can't imagine myself dead. I can't
imagine myself dying.

The Awakening by Kate Chopin

Novella
F, 30+
New Orleans, 1890s
Dramatic

Edna Pontellier, increasingly estranged from her husband, awakens to the fact that she is living not for herself but in obedience to the social roles of wife and mother dictated by 1890s New Orleans society. Here she speaks to her stockbrocker husband over dinner.

• • •

You are the embodiment of selfishness. (...) You save yourself something—I don't know what—but there is some selfish motive, and in sparing yourself you never consider for a moment what I think, or how I feel your neglect and indifference. I suppose this is what you would call unwomanly; but I have got into a habit of expressing myself. It doesn't matter to me, and you may think me unwomanly if you like. (...)

I'm spoiling your dinner, Robert; never mind what I say. You haven't eaten a morsel. (...)

Isn't this a delightful place? (...) I am so glad it has never actually been discovered. It is so quiet, so sweet, here. Do you notice there is scarcely a sound to be heard? It's so out of the way; and a good walk from the car. However, I don't mind walking. I always feel so sorry for women who don't like to walk; they miss so much—so many rare little glimpses of life; and we women learn so little of life on the whole.

"Blind Spot" from *Rules of the Lake* by Irene Ziegler

Short story
F, 30s
Florida, 1960s
Seriocomic

Lucy, a big-hearted woman with cotton candy hair and a weakness for grasshoppers (the drink, not the insect), shares her snapshots with twelve-year-old Annie at a pool hall. Lucy is secretly having an affair with Annie's father.

• • •

This is me and Tom in Las Vegas two years ago when I was president of the Tom Jones Fan Club. See, that's me. And that's Tom (...). Isn't he handsome? Oh God, and he's so nice, too, just like a regular person. You'd never know he has all that money or that women throw their underwear at him on a regular basis. Have you ever been to one of his performances? (...). Oh, you're missing something, you just don't know. First of all, they're performances see, not just concerts or whatever, because Tom really knocks himself out for his fans. He is all over that stage. I even seen him rip his pants out one time, but he was a real gentleman about it, you know? He didn't make a big thing out of it, like turn it into something dirty. He just looked kind of embarrassed, and walked off backwards, and waved and smiled that great Tom Jones smile of his, and later he came back wearing all leather pants and a jacket and high-heeled boots with rhinestones. Not everybody can pull off that look, you know, but Tom, he's not everybody. He's special. He is truly unique. Oh, here. Here he is in leather, see? (...)

Your daddy could pull that off (...). He's got the height and the build.

"Blind Spot" from *Rules of the Lake* by Irene Ziegler

Short story
F, 30s
Florida, 1960s
Seriocomic

Lucy, a big-hearted woman with cotton candy hair and a weakness for grasshoppers (the drink, not the insect), shares her snapshots with twelve-year-old Annie at a pool hall. Lucy is secretly having an affair with Annie's father.

• • •

When I was elected President of the Tom Jones Fan Club two years ago I could hardly believe this was happening to me. I mean, I had been a loyal fan club member for twelve years, but to be elected president—my heart nearly stopped. Such an honor. That summer they flew me out to Las Vegas and I met Tom Jones for the first time. Oh, it wasn't the first time I'd ever seen him—my God, I've seen his show so many times, well, I know exactly how many times, thirty-seven times I've seen his show, and I've been to Las Vegas, Atlantic City, Miami, Cincinnati, Detroit, Toledo, you name it. I've been there and I've seen Tom Jones and listened to him singing directly to me. (...)

It's his voice, you see, and that hair. That voice melts me down to a puddle right there on the floor. He just gives so much of himself to a song. Every song he sings is like he's living the words, the way he moves, the way he seeks you out of a crowd with those sad, dark eyes and says, you. You are it. You are the only one. And then I know that Jesus or Buddha or Allah are spirits whose words are something someone else wrote down on paper, but Tom Jones is alive, and he's in front of me singing, and he wants only me. (...)

Sometimes, when I think about my [late] husband, I see him singing and dancing in sexy leather pants, and pretty soon I'm not thinking about him at all anymore, and it's Tom Jones who is stroking my hair, kissing my pussy cat lips, and asking me where I put his reading glasses. Isn't that silly? Tom Jones doesn't wear glasses.

The Blue Jar by Isak Dinesan

Short story
F, 20s
England, 1942
Seriocomic

*Lady Helena, daughter of a rich old councilor to the Queen,
explains to her two old aunts why she feels she must sail,
more or less constantly.*

• • •

Nay, I have got to sail. For you must know, dear aunts, that it is all
nonsense when learned people tell you that the seas have got a
bottom to them. On the contrary, the water, which is the noblest of
the elements, does, of course, go all through the earth, so that our
planet really floats in the ether, like a soap bubble. And there, on
the other hemisphere, a ship sails, with which I have got to keep
pace. We two are like the reflection of one another, in the deep sea,
and the ship of which I speak is always exactly beneath my own
ship, upon the opposite side of the globe. You have never seen a
big fish swimming underneath a boat, following it like dark-blue
shade in the water. But in that way this ship goes, like the shadow
of my ship, and I draw it to and fro wherever I go, as the moon
draws the tides, all through the bulk of the earth. If I stopped sail-
ing, what would these poor sailors who make their bread in the
merchant service do? But I shall tell you a secret (...) In the end my
ship will go down, to the center of the globe, and at the very same
hour the other ship will sink as well—for people call it sinking,
although I can assure you that there is no up and down in the sea—
and there, in the midst of the world, we two shall meet.

The Bluest Eye by Toni Morrison

Novel
F, 30s
Lorain, Ohio, 1941
Dramatic

Pauline describes the source of her bitterness, her deep-seated conviction that she is ugly.

• • •

The onliest time I be happy seem like was when I was in the picture show. Every time I got, I went. I'd go early, before the show started. They'd cut off the lights, and everything be black. Then the screen would light up, and I'd move right on in them pictures. White men taking such good care of they women, and they all dressed up in big clean houses with the bathtubs right in the same room with the toilet. Them pictures gave me a lot of pleasure, but it made coming home hard (…). I don't know. I 'member one time I went to see Clark Gable and Jean Harlow. I fixed my hair up like I'd seen hers on a magazine. A part on the side, with one little curl on my forehead. It looked just like her. Well, almost just like. Anyway, I sat in that show with my hair done up that way and had a good time. I thought I'd see it through to the end again, and I got up to get me some candy. I was sitting back in my seat, and I taken a big bite of that candy, and it pulled a tooth right out of my mouth. I could of cried. I had good teeth, not a rotten one in my head. I don't believe I ever did get over that. There I was, five months pregnant, trying to look like Jean Harlow, and a front tooth gone. Everything went then. Look like I just didn't care no more after that. I let my hair go back, plaited it up, and settled down to just being ugly.

The Bluest Eye by Toni Morrison

Novel
F, 30s
Lorain, Ohio, 1941
Dramatic

Pauline again, first feeling nostalgic, then resigned.

• • •

When I first seed Cholly, I want you to know it was like all the bits
of color from that time down home when all us chil'ren went berry
picking after a funeral and I put some in the pocket of my Sunday
dress, and they mashed up and stained my hips. My whole dress
was messed with purple, and it never did wash out. Not the dress
nor me. I could feel that purple deep inside me. And that lemonade
Mama used to make when Pap came in out the fields. It be cool
and yellowish, with seeds floating near the bottom. And that streak
of green them june bugs made on the trees the night we left from
down home. All of them colors was in me. Just sitting there. So
when Cholly come up and tickled my foot, it was like them berries,
that lemonade, them streaks of green the june bugs made, all come
together. Cholly was thin then, with real light eyes. He used to whistle, and when I heerd him, shivers come on my skin. (...)

But it ain't like that anymore. Most times he's thrashing away inside
me before I'm woke, and through when I am. The rest of the time I
can't even be next to his stinking drunk self. But I don't care 'bout it
no more. My Maker will take care of me. I know He will. (...)
Besides, it don't make no difference about this old earth. There is
sure to be a glory. Only thing I miss sometimes is that rainbow. But
like I say, I don't recollect it much anymore.

A Boy in Winter by Maxine Chernoff

Novel
F, 30s–40s
Contemporary
Dramatic

*Nancy Horvath, a single mother with an eleven-year-old
named Danny, tries to come to terms with a tragic accident
in which Danny's friend Eddie Nova was shot through the
heart with an arrow. Frank Nova is Nancy's neighbor, with
whom she was having an affair, the person who introduced
the bow and arrow to Danny and Eddie.*

• • •

I see cars all the time with the slogan, "Guns don't kill, people do."
I see cars all the time with the slogan, "When guns are outlawed,
only outlaws will have guns." I see cars all the time with the slogan,
"Shit happens," "Practice acts of random kindness," "Save the
Whales." I want a bumper sticker that says "Save Danny." I need to
understand, though, how it happened that I need to save him, how
my son, a normal, eleven-year-old child, became newsworthy, how
Frank Nova aided and abetted my son in this process, how a com-
pound bow is fired, how it will feel if I lose Danny forever.

Sometimes I think being locked up with him would be the best solution. We could be sent away together somewhere safe. I'd still be
able to take care of him then, and I could spend all the rest of my
time figuring this out. What will Danny do in this new place, which I
imagine to be Montana, woodsy and isolated, somewhere a boy
can't meet other people and cause trouble? Watch TV, play video
games, build model gliders, collect baseball cards, tell lame jokes
that I pretend are funny, all the things he's always done: until we
met the Novas and our lives changed, first for the better and then
for the worse.

"The Bridle" from *Cathedral* by Raymond Carver

Short story
F, 40s
Contemporary
Dramatic

A forlorn woman talks while she gets a manicure at a beauty parlor.

• • •

Once, when I was in high school, a counselor asked me to come to her office. She did it with all the girls, one of us at a time. 'What dreams do you have?' this woman asked me. 'What do you see yourself doing in ten years? Twenty years?' I was sixteen or seventeen. I was just a kid. I couldn't think what to answer. I just sat there like a lump. This counselor was about the age I am now. I thought she was old. She's *old*, I said to myself. I knew her life was half over. And I felt like I knew something she didn't. Something she'd never know. A secret. Something nobody's supposed to know, or ever talk about. So I stayed quiet. I just shook my head. She must've written me off as a dope. But I couldn't say anything. You know what I mean? I thought I knew things she couldn't guess at. Now, if anybody asked me that question again, about my dreams and all, I'd tell them. (...)

I'd say, 'Dreams, you know, are what you wake up from.' That's what I'd say (...). If anybody asked, that's what I'd say. But they won't ask.

Candide by Voltaire

Novel
F, 20s
1700s
Seriocomic

Paquette was once a serving maid in a noble household. Here she is reunited with her old friend Candide and their teacher Dr. Pangloss, and she recounts her fall into prostitution.

• • •

I was very innocent when you knew me. (...) I was obliged to leave the castle shortly after His Lordship the Baron expelled you by kicking you hard and frequently in the backside. If a famous doctor had not taken pity on me I should have died. For some time I was the doctor's mistress from gratitude to him. His wife, who was madly jealous, beat me every day relentlessly; she was a fury. (...) One day, exasperated by his wife's behavior, he gave her some medicine for a little cold and it was so efficacious that she died two hours afterwards in horrible convulsions. The lady's relatives brought a criminal prosecution against the husband; he fled and I was put in prison. My innocence would not have saved me if I had not been rather pretty. The judge set me free on condition that he take the doctor's place. I was soon supplanted by a rival, expelled without a penny, and obliged to continue the abominable occupation which to you men seems so amusing and which to us is nothing but an abyss of misery. I came to Venice to practice this profession. Ah! Sir, if you could imagine what it is to be forced to caress impartially an old tradesman, a lawyer, a monk, a gondolier, an abbé; to be exposed to every insult and outrage; to be reduced often to borrow a petticoat in order to go and find some disgusting man who will lift it; to be robbed by one of what one has earned with another, to be despoiled by the police, and contemplate for the future nothing but a dreadful old age, a hospital and dunghill, you would conclude that I am one of the most unfortunate creatures in the world.

Children of the Light **by Robert Stone**

Novel
F, 30s
Contemporary
Dramatic

*About to begin shooting a movie she cares deeply about,
Lee tells her husband she wishes to stop taking her medica-
tion in order to fulfill her potential as an actress.*

• • •

Lionel, (...) it's like trying to work behind any drug—grass, Valium,
cocaine. You don't know what you're doing. You don't know what
you're like (...). I mean, (...) I can't use my eyes. I feel like a droid (...)

I want to stop (...). I want to go to work like a normal human
actress. I would like to try a little cautious experiment along the lines
of...trying to do without...for a little while (...).

We always agreed that a time would come when I would have to
try it alone (...). This is the time (...). While the kids are with you.
While I'm doing something that I feel so strong about. Man, I want
to put my pills aside and be that woman and be me (...).

Trust me, love. Trust me and I'll make you proud. It'll be me and it'll
be beautiful (...)I don't want to take them anymore (...). And be a
slave and lose my work and our sex life, a zombie. I don't want to,
Lionel.

Oh, trust me, love (...). Trust me and I'll give you something beautiful.

"Christmas Eve at Johnson's Drugs 'n' Goods" from *The Sea Birds Are Still Alive* by Toni Cade Bambara

Short story
F, Teens
Contemporary
Seriocomic

Candy cleans up at a city drugstore.

• • •

Now Uncle-Henry-type crazy is my kind of crazy. The type crazy to get you a job. He march into the "saloon" as he calls it and tells Leon D that he is not an equal-opportunity employer and that he, Alderman Henry Peoples, is going to put some fire to his ass. So soon's summer comes, me and Madeen got us a job at Leon D. Salon. (...)

Madeen got fired right off on account of the pound of mascara she wears on each lash and them weird dresses she designs for herself (with less than a yard of cloth each if you ask me). I did my best to hang in there so's me and Madeen'd have hang-around money (...).

But to hear Uncle Henry tell it, writing about it all to Daddy, I was working at a promising place making a name for myself. And Aunt Harriet listening to Uncle Henry read the letter, looking me up and down and grunting. She know what kind of name it must be, cause my name in the family is Miss Clumsy. Like if you got a glass-top coffee table with doodads on 'em, or a hurricane lamp sitting on a mantel anywhere near a door I got to come through, or an antique jar you brought all the way from Venice the time you won the cross-word puzzle contest—you can rest assure I'll demolish them by and by. I ain't vicious, I'm just clumsy. It's my gawky stage, Mama says.

Clear Springs by Bobbie Ann Mason

Memoir
F, 20+
Kentucky, 1954
Dramatic

*A daughter recalls a thwarted dream she and her mother
shared.*

• • •

I was so excited I couldn't sleep. Running our own little restaurant
could mean we wouldn't have to work in the garden. I wanted
nothing more to do with okra and beans. Besides, the restaurant
had an apartment above it. I wanted to live there, on the highway.
Marlene was still running her frozen-custard stand nearby, and now
I too would get to meet strangers traveling through. Mama and I
inspected the apartment(...) It was all new and fresh. I loved it(...)

Mama had to give up the restaurant even before the trial period
ended. She didn't do it voluntarily. Granddaddy stepped in and told
her she had to.

"We need you here at home," he said. "Running a eating place out
on the highway ain't fitten work."

Daddy didn't stand up for her. "How would you make anything?"
he asked her. "By the time you pay out that hundred dollars a
month and all the expenses, you won't have nothing left. First thing
you know, you'll get behind and then you'll be owing *him.*"

Granny said, "And who's going to do your cooking here?"

That was that. Afterward, Mama cooked her hamburger platters at
home, but they weren't the same without the fountain Cokes and
the jukebox and the television. I thought I saw a little fire go out of
her then. Much later, her fire would almost die. But my own flame
was burning brighter. I had had a glimpse of life outside the farm,
and I wanted it.

Coming Attractions by Fannie Flagg

Novel
F, 17
Mississippi, 1958
Comic

Daisy Fay gets a glimpse of the Bohemian life.

• • •

Yesterday Mr. Cecil took me over to meet a friend of his who is a sculptress and comes from a very rich family, but has been disowned. Her name is Paris Knights. She's beautiful and uses a black cigarette holder and wears army pants with pearls. She also takes snuff and cusses like a sailor. Paris is very sophisticated if you ask me.

You should see her sculptures. I know what they are, I'm not dumb, hundreds of men's things of all sizes. The reason she got disowned was because she donated one to the Hattiesburg Museum of Art to be auctioned off at a big Beaux Arts Ball. One of the women on the committee thought she recognized her husband's thing and threw a martini in Paris's face and caused a big upset. Paris said the resemblance was just wishful thinking on that woman's part. (...)

When Paris asked me if I believed in free love, I didn't know what to say, so I said yes. She's had affairs with all kinds of men, including Orientals. She thinks I am at the age where I should be experiencing life. To tell you the truth, I think I'd better wait. I haven't even gone to bed with an American man yet. She's looking for an apprentice to help her in her studio, but I don't feel like handling those sculptures of hers. Maybe Catholic school has made me a prude.

Cruising Paradise by Sam Shepard

Short story
F, 40+
Southwest, 1960s
Seriocomic

Aunt Mellie gives her teenage nephew and his buddy a good talking to.

• • •

Don't you characters drink any a that beer in there! That beer's gotta last me two days! (...)

Every now and then you might just give a thought to the other person, ya know! Wouldn't hurt. Wouldn't kill you a bit to be a little thoughtful! (...) Same problem with yer old man! That musta been where you picked it up. Same lack of consideration. Never had a thought for the other person. Not one notion (...). He just went his merry way, didn't he! Didn't give one hoot in hell about the consequences. Not to say that he ever did have any kind of future. Snakebit sonofabitch. Didn't surprise me one bit the way he passed. He deserved every inch of it. You think that's hard? I suppose you think I'm bein' hard, huh? (...) Well, nothin' was as hard as yer old man! The things he put yer mother through. It's a wonder she lived as long as she did. And all the damn excuses he had for his behavior. I never met a man with more excuses. Same as you! Excuses, excuses! What's yer big excuse tonight, Crewlaw! Answer me that! (...)

Stumblin' in here, middle of the damn night, and stealin' my beer! I know what yer doin' in there. (...)

Stay outa that icebox, Crewlaw!

"Daughter to Mother" from *The Bad-Tempered Man* or *The Misanthrope* by Menander, translated by Philip Vellacott

Poem
F, Teens/20s
Ancient Greece
Dramatic

A daughter challenges her mother's regard for class and race.

• • •

Family? I'm fed up with this talk of "family."
Mother, don't—if you love me—everytime I mention
A man, start talking about his family. People who
Haven't a single good quality to call their own—
They are the ones who talk like that of family.
Or titles, or decorations; reel off grandfathers
One after the other, and that's all they've got. Can you
Tell me of a man who hasn't got grandfathers? or how
A man could be born without them? People who, for one
Reason or another—living abroad, or losing friends—
Can't name their grandfathers—are they any worse both than those
Who can? Mother, if a man has a noble character
Which prompts him to a good life, then he's of noble birth,
Even if he's a black African. And you "don't like
Scythians"? To hell!

"Dead on the Road" from *Mama Makes Up Her Mind* by Bailey White

Essay
F, 30s/40s
Contemporary South
Comic

Bailey White shares an anecdote about her mother.

• • •

My mother eats things she finds dead on the road. Her standards are high. She claims she won't eat anything that's not a fresh kill. But I don't trust her. I require documentation. I won't eat it unless she can tell me the model and tag number of the car that struck it.

Mama is an adventurous and excellent cook, and we have feasted not only on doves, turkeys, and quail, but robins, squirrels, and, only once, a possum. I draw the line at snakes. (...)

We have a prissy aunt Eleanor who comes to dinner every third Friday. We always get out the linen and polish the silver when she comes. She expects it. Last month we sat her down to an elegant meal, complete with the Spode china and camellias in a crystal bowl.

"The quail are delicious," my aunt sighed. "And I haven't found a single piece of shot. How do you manage it?"

"Intersection of 93 and Baggs Road," recites Mama. "Green late model pickup, Florida tag. Have another one. And some rice, El."

"The Dead" from *Dubliners* by James Joyce

Novella
F, 30s/40s
Dublin, 1910s
Dramatic

Gretta remembers a boy she knew as a teenager and relates the story to her husband, Gabriel.

• • •

I think he died for me (...) It was in the winter, (she said,) about the beginning of the winter when I was going to leave my grandmother's and come up here to the convent. And he was ill at the time in his lodgings in Galway and wouldn't be let out and his people in Oughterard were written to. He was in decline, they said, or something like that. I never knew rightly. (...) Poor fellow, (she said). He was very fond of me and he was such a gentle boy. We used to go out together, walking, you know, Gabriel, like the way they do in the country. He was going to study singing only for his health. He had a very good voice, poor Michael Furey. (...)

And then when it came to the time for me to leave Galway and come up to the convent he was much worse and I wouldn't be let see him so I wrote a letter saying I was going up to Dublin and would be back in the summer and hoping he would be better then. (...)

Then the night before I left I was in my grandmother's house in Nuns' Island, packing up, and I heard gravel thrown up against the window. The window was so wet I couldn't see so I ran downstairs as I was and slipped out the back into the garden and there was the poor fellow at the end of the garden, shivering. (...)

I implored of him to go home at once and told him he would get his death in the rain. But he said he did not want to live. I can see his eyes as well as well! (...) He went home. And when I was only a week in the convent he died and he was buried in Oughterard where his people came from. O, the day I heard that, that he was dead!

"The First Dance, 1975" by Irene Zahava

Short story
F, 30+
Contemporary
Seriocomic

A woman recalls a particularly memorable dance partner.

• • •

I had recently moved from the Bronx to Brooklyn. I saw a flyer in the laundromat, advertising a dance at Barnard College, so I took the subway up to 116th and Broadway. I didn't know anyone there. I stood in the corner where the shadows were deepest but a woman sought me out and asked me to dance. I was too terrified to say no so I said OK. Her head was completely shaven—she was 100 percent bald without a trace of hair on her smooth and glistening scalp. I noticed this at almost the same moment I saw she wasn't wearing a shirt. I tried not to stare at her breasts. I stared at her bald head, instead. It struck me that I was dancing with a three-breasted woman. This was not a particularly comforting or amusing thought. Eventually, the band took a break and we stopped dancing. I thanked her, excused myself politely, and quickly walked away. I went back to the shadows in the corner and stayed another five minutes. Then I took a taxi back to Park Slope.

"For Bo" from *Cowboys Are My Weakness* by Pam Houston

Short story
F, 20s
Colorado, 1990
Seriocomic

The speaker reflects fondly on family and fresh starts.

• • •

The first Saturday in May is more than just Kentucky Derby Day at our house. Each year since we've been married we watch the Derby, get a little stupid on Kentucky bourbon, and head for the dog pound. It's become a three-year tradition, and if we hadn't lost Hazel to cancer last winter, we'd be going on dog number four.

Another tradition in our house is to spend at least half of every weekend in bed, and Sam finishes the porch and joins me under the covers. Sam says our gravestones will read: "They never had a lot of money, but they always had a lot of sex." You can probably understand why my mother doesn't like Sam. She gets most of her information from my Aunt Colleen, who moved out here several years ago. Colleen's got lots of money and very little imagination. Last time they talked, she told my mother that one of these days I would wake up and realize that squalor is not enough, and now my mother is holding her breath. Colleen's an attractive woman for her age, but her hair is always stiff, and a lot of her clothes have comic-strip characters printed on them. Sam says she shouldn't knock squalor till she's tried it.

I've invited Colleen to dinner today too. Sam thinks I'm asking for trouble, but I try to do what I can for my family. Besides, Colleen offered to drive my mother to and from the airport, which means I won't have to watch her cry.

Fried Green Tomatoes at the Whistle Stop Café by Fannie Flagg

Novel
F, 80s
Alabama. Contemporary
Seriocomic

Cleo Threadgoode chats with a younger woman who sits next to her at the Rose Terrace nursing home, in Birmingham, Alabama.

• • •

Now, you ask me the year somebody got married . . . who they married . . . or what the bride's mother wore, and nine times out of ten I can tell you, but for the life of me, I cain't tell you when it was I got to be so old. It just sorta slipped up on me. The first time I noticed it was June of this year, when I was in the hospital for my gallbladder, which they still have, or maybe they threw it out by now . . . who knows. That heavyset nurse had just given me another one of those Fleet enemas they're so fond of over there when I noticed what they had on my arm. It was a white band that said: Mrs. Cleo Threadgoode . . . an eighty-six-year-old woman. Imagine that!

When I got back home, I told my friend Mrs. Otis, I guess the only thing left for us to do is to sit around and get ready to croak . . . She said she preferred the term pass over to the other side. Poor thing, I didn't have the heart to tell her that no matter what you call it, we're all gonna croak, just the same . . . .

Gertrude and Claudius
by John Updike

Novel
F, 30s–40s
Elizabethan satire
Dramatic

Gertrude has a late night talk with Claudius about her troubled son, Hamlet.

• • •

He is too charmed by himself. He has no need for you or me. (...)

I am his mother, yes. I know him. He is cold. You are not, Claudius. You are warm, like me. You crave action. You want to live, to seize the day. To my son, everything is mockery, a show. He is the only man in his universe. If there are other people with feelings, then that just makes the show more lively, he might concede. Even I, who love him as a mother cannot help doing, from that moment when they place the cause of your pain in your arms, itself wailing and whimpering in memory of the joint ordeal—even me he views disdainfully, as evidence of his natural origins, and proof that his father succumbed to concupiscence. (...)

Hamlet wants to feel, I believe, and to be an actor on a stage outside his teeming head, but cannot as yet.

"Gertrude Talks Back" from *Good Bones and Simple Murders* by Margaret Atwood

Short story
F, 30s–40s
Elizabethan satire
Comic

Queen Gertrude tells Hamlet the real truth.

• • •

I always thought it was a mistake, calling you Hamlet. I mean, what kind of a name is that for a young boy? It was your father's idea. (...)

I wanted to call you George.

I am *not* wringing my hands, I'm drying my nails. (...)

I *know* your father was handsomer than Claudius (...). But handsome isn't everything, especially in a man, and far be it from me to speak ill of the dead, but I think it's about time I pointed out to you that your dad just wasn't a whole lot of fun. Noble, sure, I grant you. But Claudius, well, he likes a drink now and then. He appreciates a decent meal. He enjoys a laugh, know what I mean? You don't always have to be tiptoeing around because of some holier-than-thou principle or something.

Some days I think it would have been better for both of us if you hadn't been an only child. But you realize who you have to thank for that. You have no idea what I used to put up with. And every time I felt like a little, you know, just to warm up my aging bones, it was like I'd suggested murder.

Oh! You think *what*? You think Claudius murdered your Dad? Well, no wonder you've been so rude to him at the dinner table!

If I'd known that, I could have put you straight in no time flat.

It wasn't Claudius, darling.

It was me.

The Giant's House
by Elizabeth McCracken

Novel
F, 26
Cape Cod, 1950
Seriocomic

Peggy, no ordinary reference librarian, defends her career choice.

• • •

People think librarians are unromantic, unimaginative. This is not true (...). The idea of a library full of books, the books full of knowledge, fills me with fear and love and courage and endless wonder. (...)

Unromantic? This is a reference librarian's fantasy.

A patron arrives, says, Tell me something. You reach across the desk and pull him toward you, bear hug him a second and then take him into your lap, stroke his forehead, whisper facts in his ear. *The climate of Chad is tropical in the south, desert in the north. Source: 1991 CIA World Factbook. Do you love me? Americans consumed 6.2 gallons of tea per capita in 1989. Source: Statistical Abstract of the United States.* Synecdoche *is a literary device meaning the part for the whole, as in, the crowned heads of Europe. I love you. I could find you British Parliamentary papers, I could track down a book you only barely remember reading. Do you love me now? We own that book, we subscribe to that journal, Elvis Presley's first movie was called* Love Me Tender.

And then you lift the patron again, take him over the desk and set him down so gently he doesn't feel it, because there's someone else arriving, and she looks, oh, she looks *uninformed.*

"Glory Goes and Gets Some"
by Emily Carter

Short story
F, 35
Contemporary
Seriocomic

Gloria Bronski places an ad in the Personals column of Positive People.

• • •

I hate the word horny, redolent as it is of yellowed calluses and pizza-crust bunions, but there you go. Sober for eighteen months, I'd been giving up my will to God and practicing the three m's— meetings, meditation, masturbation. But no matter the electronic reinforcement, it gets old mashing the little pink button all by your lonesome, night after night. Now here's the dilemma I'm staring at: "I AM HIV POSITIVE, WHO WILL HAVE SEX WITH ME?" If I was a guy it might be different, but carrying around the eve of destruction between my creamy white thighs doesn't exactly make me feel like a sex goddess. But I can't possibly be the only positive heterosexual recovering drug addict on huge amounts of Prozac in the universe. And of course, as it turned out, I wasn't. As they tell you in Treatment, don't wear yourself out with Terminal Uniqueness. Another kitchy-coo catchphrase that turns out, finally, to have the distinctly unsamplerlike ring of truth.

The problem was the research. I hate doing it, I hate thinking about doing it, I hate, with every fiber of my being, the process of going to libraries, making phone calls, looking things up, writing them down. Especially on this particular topic, which I'd rather not think about to begin with. But there you go, no stick, no carrot, if you get my drift. I found what I was looking for with very little trouble, as a matter of fact, a magazine called *Positive People,* and I put in my ad: Female, 35, hetero. Permanent graduate student. Red hair, green eyes. You: neither sociopath nor systems analyst. Will consider anything in between.

Half a Life by Jill Ciment

Memoir
F, 20s
Contemporary New York
Seriocomic

Karen, a model, explains the tricks of the soft porn photo trade.

• • •

You wait for a 'photographer' to come in; then you wait for the jerk to choose you. The guys usually bring their own equipment, but if they don't, Eddie rents them a Polaroid and flash. He also sells film at outrageous prices. Some of the girls keep film in their pockets and, when Eddie's not looking, try to underbid him.

Most of the photographers are just harmless losers who would probably faint if you touched them. But if some freak tries to grope you, you scream for Eddie. There's a strip of masking tape in front of each stage and it's a no-no for the men to cross it, but you can sometimes earn a big tip letting a guy take a sleazoid close-up. (...)

The guys are obsessed with choosing the right girl for the right scenery. I guess that's the creative part. I'm always picked for the Valentine Room. They pretend to be all interested in the artsy-fartsy stuff like lighting and angle and mood. Then, like...da...it just dawned on them, they ask you to spread your legs a little wider. (...)

The trick is to get regulars. They tip the best and they're nicer, a lot nicer. Once in a blue moon, a real photographer drops in. Eddie told me that last year one of his girls got in *Penthouse*. She was the centerfold and everything. I mean, you never know.

Hard Times by Charles Dickens

Novel
F, 20s
England, 1854
Dramatic

Louisa, eldest child of Mr. and Mrs. Thomas Gradgrind, wife of Josiah Bounderby, tells her father precisely what being reared by "fact" and "reason" have cost her.

• • •

Father, you have trained me from my cradle? (...)

I curse the hour in which I was born to such a destiny. (...)

How could you give me life, and take from me all the inappreciable things that raise it from the state of conscious death? Where are the graces of my soul? Where are the sentiments of my heart? What have you done, oh, Father, what have you done, with the garden that should have bloomed once, in this great wilderness here? *(Strikes herself with both hands upon her bosom...)* (...)

I don't reproach you, Father. What you have never nurtured in me, you have never nurtured in yourself; but oh! if you had only done so, long ago, or if you had only neglected me, what a much better and much happier creature I should have been this day! (...)

Father, if you had known, when we were last together here, what even I feared while I strove against it—as it has been my task from infancy to strive against every natural prompting that has arisen in my heart; if you had known that there lingered in my breast sensibilities, affections, weaknesses capable of being cherished into strength, defying all the calculations ever made by man, and no more known to his arithmetic than his Creator is—would you have given me to the husband whom I am now sure that I hate?(...)

"Help Me Find My Spaceman Lover" from *Tabloid Dreams* by Robert Olen Butler

Short story
F, 30s/40s
Bovary, Alabama. Contemporary
Comic

A woman explains her attraction to a spaceman.

• • •

I never thought I could fall for a spaceman. I mean, you see them in the newspaper and they kind of give you the willies, all skinny and hairless and wiggly looking, and if you touched one, even to shake hands, you just know it would be like when you were about fifteen (...) and it was the first time ever that you touched (...) well, you know what I'm talking about. Anyway, that's what it's always seemed like to me with spacemen, and most everybody around here feels about the same way, I'm sure. (...)

Take my daddy. When I showed him a few years ago in the newspaper how a spaceman had endorsed Bill Clinton for president and they had a picture of a spaceman standing there next to Bill Clinton—without any clothes on, by the way—the spaceman, that is, not Bill Clinton, though I wouldn't put it past him, to tell the truth (...). But I showed my daddy the newspaper (...), and he snorted and said that he wasn't surprised people like that was supporting the Democrats (...), and I said no, Daddy, he's a spaceman, and he said people like that don't even look human, and I said no, Daddy, he's not human, and my daddy said, that's what I'm saying, make him get a job.

But I did fall for a spaceman, as it turned out, fell pretty hard. I met him in the parking lot at the twenty-four-hour Wal-Mart.

"His Heart Shares in His Proportions" from *The Giant's House* by Elizabeth McCracken

Novel
F, 50+
A small New England town. Contemporary
Dramatic

Peggy is a retired librarian. The love of her life, a young man half her age and more than twice her size, has died, prematurely, of Giantism.

• • •

I want to tell you about his body.

I want to describe his feet, (...) size thirty-seven, triple A. The store in Hyannis still made his shoes. I'd had to call and ask them to rush and make a new pair to replace the old ones, and they told me how to measure everything (...). I did it regularly. We set his foot down on paper—not typing paper, which was too small, but some stuff cut from a roll at an artists' supply shop, and traced. I did this. His feet left damp marks on the paper; his second toes were longer than his big toes, and I wondered whether this was a sign of some- thing, either in medicine or folk wisdom.

His calves were unmuscled things. I know because I held on to them while I traced. This was late in the day, eight-thirty or so—we wanted to get his feet at their highest swollen ebb—and I'd slipped my hands up under his pant cuff to hold on.

His thighs—

I want to say that they were like railroad ties, and they were, they were solid and blocky and no wider at the hip than at the knee, but I promised myself I wouldn't turn his body into something it wasn't, I wouldn't compare it to other things. People always did that. They made him into a redwood tree, a building, the Eiffel Tower. (...)

I want to say, *his body was just a man's body, only bigger. His thighs were the thighs you have met before in your life, but longer. It was any body you've ever known; there was just more of it.*

"Hitchhiker in Pillbox Hat with Net" by Lou Robinson

Short story
F, 20s
A car. Contemporary
Comic

A hitchhiker bends the ear of her driver.

• • •

I was wondering if anyone would pick me up or if someone would pick me up and kill me, but I think my vibes are too good for that since I stopped being depressed. I was really depressed last week, I used to think about killing myself a lot, like from a doorknob or something, but all the ways you can kill yourself are too painful, know what I mean. I guess if you're too depressed to do anything, killing yourself is just too much work. Anyway I decided to stop being depressed because it was so boring talking about myself all the time. I mean when I was depressed I would have gotten into this car and started telling you all about how I lost $500, my rent, and I don't have a place to live and everything. I was hoping to get in the car and hear a lot of interesting things from you that I could think about for a change. Drop me off at the bus station I'm going to Toronto to be an actress. When I was depressed I used to look terrible but since I stopped I've been dressing up. I've been looking good for about two weeks now. I don't know if I can keep it up. Gloves, hat, colors—I make sure I wear some color, salmon or lime or lemon—food colors, you know. You should wear some color yourself, you wouldn't just eat black things would you?

The House on Mango Street
by Sandra Cisneros

Novel
F, Teens
Hispanic quarter of Chicago. Contemporary
Dramatic

*Esperanza Cordero rails against her friend Sally for "deceiv-
ing" her about the realities of sex.*

• • •

Sally, Sally a hundred times. Why didn't you hear me when I called?
Why didn't you tell them to leave me alone? The one who grabbed
me by the arm, he wouldn't let me go. He said I love you, Spanish
girl, I love you, and pressed his sour mouth into mine. (...)

Why did you leave me all alone? I waited my whole life. You're a
liar. They all lied. All the books and magazines, everything that told
it wrong. Only his dirty fingernails against my skin, only his sour
smell again. The moon that watched. The tilt-a-whirl. The red
clowns laughing their thick-tongue laugh.

Then the colors began to whirl. Sky tipped. Their high black gym
shoes ran. Sally, you lied, you lied. He wouldn't let me go. He said I
love you, I love you, Spanish girl.

How the Garcia Girls Lost Their Accents
by Julia Alvarez

Novel
F, 40s/50s
Bronx, New York. Contemporary
Seriocomic

Mami, a Spanish Caribbean society matron in exile in the Bronx, explains to a doctor why she and her husband are committing their daughter to a private mental hospital.

• • •

It started with that crazy diet (...). At first, she looked good. She had let herself get a little plump, and with her fine bones Sandi can't carry extra weight (...). Then, she went away to a graduate program, so we didn't see her for awhile. (...)

So one day we get this call. The dean. She says she doesn't want to alarm us, but could we come down immediately. Our daughter is in the hospital, too weak to do anything. All she does is read. (...)

We took the next plane, and when we got there, I didn't recognize my own daughter. Sandi was a toothpick. (...)

She had lists and lists of books to read (...). Finally she told us why she couldn't stop reading. She didn't have much time left. She had to read all the great works of man because soon...soon she wouldn't be human. (...)

She told us that she was being turned out of the human race. She was becoming a monkey (...). A monkey! my baby! (...)

One morning, I go in her room to wake her up, and I find her lying in bed and looking up at her hands (...). I call her name, Sandi!, and she keeps turning her hands, this way, that, and staring at them. I scream at her to answer me, and she doesn't even look at me. Nothing. And she's making these awful sounds like she's a zoo. (...)

And my Sandi holds up her hands to me (…). And she screams, *Monkey hands, monkey hands.*

"I Am Candy Jones"
by Gary Indiana

Short story
F, 40+
Contemporary
Seriocomic

Candy/Mildred suffers from multiple personalities. She grew up in Reno, Nevada, where she worked for many years as an accountant at a Korean vegetable company.

•   •   •

I am Candy Jones. I am also Mildred Huxley. (...)

It was the 60s, and you know what they were. I was blonde, busty, and bored in accounting school, though I hasten to say I was by no means miserable. Au contraire, Miss Popularity would only begin to describe the way heads would turn when I walked through the corridors of the Samuel Fuller School of Accounting on La Cienega Boulevard. We were not far from Hollywood High, and a list of hunky dudes I dated then would make *Seventeen* look like *Good Housekeeping*. I'm not bragging but complaining: I couldn't keep the boys off me, and what was even worse, I was becoming radicalized.

That's right. Me, Candy Jones, or rather I, Candy Jones, beehive princess, was caught up in the whirl of events we now think of as the 60s. I went on marches. I signed petitions. I demonstrated. Now when I look back on it all I still think it was the right thing to do at the time. But the tragedy is, you see, that when this kind of idea comes over me now, I'm never quite sure that it isn't Mildred talking. Mildred who has my big hair, my large eyes, my breasts and all the rest of all that. Mildred whose voice is different than mine; I have heard on the tape-recorder recordings my husband, Dick Bridgely, has made of Mildred's voice, coming out of my, Candy Jones's, mouth. Mildred would never go on marches.

"I Stand Here Ironing" from *Tell Me a Riddle* by Tillie Olsen

Short story
F, 40+
Urban America, 1960
Dramatic

The mother of a nineteen-year-old responds to a college counselor's request that she "manage the time to come in and talk with me about your daughter."

• • •

She is so lovely. Why did you want me to come in at all? Why were you concerned? She will find her way. (...)

I will never total it all. I will never come in to say: She was a child seldom smiled at. Her father left me before she was a year old. I had to work her first six years when there was work, or I sent her home and to his relatives. There were years she had care she hated. She was dark and thin and foreign-looking in a world where the prestige went to blondness and curly hair and dimples, she was slow where glibness was prized. She was a child of anxious, not proud, love. We were poor and could not afford for her the soil of easy growth. I was a young mother, I was a distracted mother. There were the other children pushing up, demanding. Her younger sister seemed all that she was not. There were years she did not want me to touch her. She kept too much in herself, her life was such she had to keep too much in herself. My wisdom came too late. She has much to her and probably little will come of it. She is a child of her age, of depression, of war, of fear.

Let her be. So all that is in her will not bloom—but in how many does it? There is still enough left to live by. Only help her to know—help make it so there is cause for her to know—that she is more than this dress on the ironing board, helpless before the iron.

"In Response to Executive Order 9066: All Americans of Japanese Descent Must Report to Relocation Centers" by Dwight Okita

Poem
F, 14
Western USA, World War II
Dramatic

The poet's mother spent World War II in a relocation center. Over 100,000 Americans of Japanese descent were, without due process, forced into these centers during this time.

• • •

Dear Sirs:
Of course I'll come. I've packed my galoshes
and three packets of tomato seeds. Janet calls them
"love apples." My father says where we're going
they won't grow.

I am a fourteen-year-old girl with bad spelling
and a messy room. If it helps any, I will tell you
I have always felt funny using chopsticks
and my favorite food is hot dogs.
My best friend is a white girl named Denise—
we look at boys together. She sat in front of me
all through grade school because of our names:
O'Connor, Ozawa. I know the back of Denise's head very well.
I tell her she's going bald. She tells me I copy on tests.
We're best friends.

I saw Denise today in Geography class.
She was sitting on the other side of the room.
"You're trying to start a war," she said, "giving secrets away
to the Enemy, Why can't you keep your big mouth shut?"

I didn't know what to say.
I gave her a packet of tomato seeds
and asked her to plant them for me, told her
when the first tomato ripened
she'd miss me.

Independence Day by Richard F‹

Novel
F, 40s
Contemporary
Dramatic

Unhappily remarried, Ann talks about past hurts to her ex-husband, who still loves her.

• • •

You like thinking I ought to be sorry I married Charley. But I'm not sorry. Not at all (...). He's a much better person than you are (...), not that you have any reason to believe that, since you don't know him. He even has a good opinion of you. He tries to be a pal to these children. He thinks we've done a better than average job with them (...). He's nice to me. He tells the truth. He's faithful. (...)

Frank, you know when we were all living down in Haddam five years ago, in that sick little arrangement you thrived on, and you were fucking that little Texas bimbo and having the time of your life, I actually put an ad in the *Pennysaver,* advertising myself as a woman who seeks male companionship. I actually risked boredom and rape just to keep things the way you like them. (...)

I divorced you (...)because I didn't like you. And I didn't like you because I didn't trust you. Do you think you ever told me the truth once, the whole truth? (...)

Some things just can't be fixed later, can they?

ntimacy" from *Where I'm Calling From* by Raymond Carver

Short story
F, 40s
Contemporary
Dramatic

When her ex-husband drops by, the narrator serves him a cup of coffee and a good piece of her mind.

• • •

After that time, when you went away, nothing much mattered after that. Not the kids, not God, not anything. It was like I didn't know what hit me. It was like I had *stopped living*. My life had been going along, going along, and then it just stopped (...). I thought, If I'm not worth anything to him, well, I'm not worth anything to myself or anybody else either. That was the worst thing I felt. I thought my heart would break. What am I saying? It did break. Of course it broke. It broke, just like that. It's still broke, if you want to know. And so there you have it in a nutshell. My eggs in one basket (...). A tisket, a tasket. All my rotten eggs in one basket. (...)

You found somebody else for yourself, didn't you? It didn't take long. And you're happy now. (...)

Listen, I know your heart, mister. I always did. I knew it back then, and I know it now. I know your heart inside and out, and don't you ever forget it. Your heart is a jungle, a dark forest, it's a garbage pail, if you want to know. (...)

Honey, no offense, but sometimes I think I could shoot you and watch you kick.

Kitchen by Banana Yoshimoto, translated by Megan Backus

Novel
F/M, 50s
Contemporary
Seriocomic

*Eriko, a transsexual nightclub owner, is the father of the
20-something Yuichi, to whom s/he speaks—in a written
"will"—here.*

• • •

Yuichi, think about what I'm about to say. If I should die, you will be
left all alone. But you have Mikage, don't you? I'm not joking about
that girl. We have no relatives. When I married your mother, her
family cut off relations entirely. And then, when I became a woman,
they cursed me. So I'm asking you, DON'T, whatever you do, DO
NOT contact them, ever. Do you understand me?

Yes, Yuichi, in this world there are all kinds of people. There are
people who choose to live their lives in filth; this is hard for me to
understand. People who purposely do abhorrent things, just for the
attention it draws to them, until they themselves are trapped. I cannot understand it, and no matter how much they suffer I cannot
feel pity for them. But I have cheerfully chosen to make my body my
fortune. I am *beautiful!* I am *dazzling!* If people I don't care for are
attracted to me, I accept it as the wages of beauty. So, if I should be
killed, it will be an accident. Don't get any strange ideas. Believe in
the me that you knew. (...)

Call the lawyer, ok? In any case, I've left everything to you except
the club. Isn't it great being an only child?

Larry's Party by Carol Shields

Novel
F, 40s
Contemporary
Seriocomic

After one sad early marriage, Midge is living in North Toronto with a fifty-year-old "designer of sidewalk hoardings." They've been together eight years. Here she defends her relationship to her brother, Larry.

• • •

Perfect is not what I'm after (...). I know that at my age there're bound to be compromises. For one thing, I never really fancied pressing my tender lips up against a mustache (...). Actually, though, there's not all that much pressing between Ian and me these days. Of any kind. I don't think he's seeing anyone else during the day, but I wouldn't rule it out. How do I stand not knowing? Because I'm busy as hell down at the store, that's how. I get home from work, and Ian's got something in the oven, usually something decent, and he's got the table set, sort of, and I can, you know, put my feet up (...). He's already patted out our potato patches on the couch and we just fall into them for the evening, a kind of TV trance that isn't as bad as you might think. At least he isn't forever switching channels, that's one thing in his favor. And what else?—let me think. Oh, God, what else? He goes fishing now and then so that I get the house to myself, and is that ever heaven! (...) Hmmmm. When he's got money he spends it. One tight-fisted man was enough for me (...). Ian understands the worth of a good bottle of wine. He knows chocolate from chocolate. He doesn't gobble peanuts or pretzels, any of that stuff, and he gets his teeth attended to twice a year. Now that's enough to build a relationship on, don't you think?

"Late August" from *Selected Poems 1965–1975* by Margaret Atwood

Poem
F, 20+
1975
Dramatic

A lover invokes the languid sweetness of late summer.

• • •

This is the plum season, the nights
blue and distended, the moon
hazed, this is the season of peaches

with their lush lobed bulbs
that glow in the dusk, apples
that drop and rot
sweetly, their brown skins veined as glands

No more the shrill voices
that cried Need Need
from the cold pond, bladed
and urgent as new grass

Now it is the crickets
that say Ripe Ripe
slurred in the darkness while the plums

dripping on the lawn outside
our window, burst
with a sound like thick syrup
muffled and slow

The air is still
warm, flesh moves over
flesh, there is no
hurry

Leaving Las Vegas
by John O'Brien

Novel
F, 29
Contemporary
Dramatic

*Sera, a prostitute, discovers some profound connection with
Ben, a man intent on destroying himself with alcohol.*

• • •

We were sitting at the bar talking about blackjack. You seemed just
fine—a little drunker than usual, but nothing really strange. Then I
noticed your head start to droop, so I put my hand on your shoulder. Wham! You swung your arm at me and jumped back, falling
off the barstool and crashing into a cocktail waitress (...) there was a
terrible mess. You were yelling *Fuck*! over and over again, very loudly.
I tried to shut you up and help you to your feet, but you kept
swinging at me—not so much like you wanted to hit me, but more
just waving me away. Security was there by then and you stopped
yelling when you saw them(...). Things started to settle down, and I
talked them into letting me walk you out (...). I also promised that
you would never walk in there again. (...)

Anyway, we got home, you made us some drinks, and ten minutes
later you were asleep on the floor. (...)

Here's my speech. I know that this shouldn't be acceptable to me,
but it is. Don't ask me to explain. Maybe I'm not doing what I
should be, but I think I'm doing what you need me to do. I sense
that your trouble is very big, and I'm scared for you. But falling
down in a casino is little stuff. It doesn't bother me. It has nothing
to do with us. (...)

I'm just using you. I need you. Can we not talk about it anymore.
Please, not another word, okay?

"A Lesson" by Jill McCorkle from *Three Minutes or Less: Life Lessons from America's Greatest Writers*

Essay
F, 20+
Contemporary
Seriocomic

A woman relates where she learned to be so cautious.

• • •

[M]y dad, a man who was the king of "what if." (...)

I was once in a hotel room in Georgia with my parents, and I happened to look off to the side, where my dad had gone out on the balcony to smoke his pipe and I noticed that two legs of his chair were out on the balcony and two were in the room, and I went over and I said, "Are you coming or going?" and he said, "Well, you know, I was all the way out there and then I started thinking, What if the guy who was responsible for my balcony was having a bad day. What if he was depressed, alcoholic? Maybe he was just having a bad morning and he forgot to insert the steel beams in the right places." He said, "This way, if this balcony starts to shake at all, all I have to do is tilt my chair backward and I'll land safely in the room."

Needless to say I've always read the card on the airplanes and always know where the fire exit is.

The Liar's Club by Mary Karr

Memoir
F, 20+
Texas, 1961
Dramatic

While writing her past, a victim of child sexual abuse
attacks her attacker.

• • •

I was seven and a good ten years from anything like breasts. My
school record says I weighed about fifty pounds. Think of two good-
sized Smithfield hams—that's roughly how big I was. Then think of
a newly erect teenaged boy on top of that and pumping between
my legs. It couldn't have taken very long.

(I picture him now reading this, and long to reach out of the page
and grab ahold of his shirt front that we might together reminisce
some. Hey, bucko. Probably you don't read, but you must have
somebody who reads for you—your pretty wife or some old neighbor boy you still go fishing with. Where will you be when the news
of this paragraph floats back to you? For some reason, I picture you
changing your wife's tire. She'll mention that in some book I wrote,
somebody from the neighborhood is accused of diddling me at
seven. Maybe your head will click back a notch as this registers.
Maybe you'll see your face's image spread across the silver hubcap
as though it's been flattened by a ballpeen hammer. Probably you
thought I forgot what you did, or you figured it was no big deal. I
say this now across decades and thousands of miles solely to remind
you of the long memory my daddy always said I had.)

When he was done with me it was full dark. I unballed my clothes
and tried to brush off any insects. He helped me to pull them on
and tied my Keds for me. He washed me off at the faucet that
came out of the side of somebody's house. The water was warm
from being in the pipe on a hot day, and my legs were still sticky
after.

The Liar's Club by Mary Karr

Memoir
F, 20+
Texas, 1961
Seriocomic

Mary Marlene recalls how she learned, as a child, to elicit pity from grown-ups for her own purposes.

• • •

I had this succinct way of explaining the progression of my grand-mother's cancer to neighbor ladies who asked: "First, they took off her toenail, then her toe, then her foot. Then they shot mustard gas through her leg till it was burnt black, and she screamed for six weeks nonstop. Then they took off her leg, and it was like a black stump laid up on a pillow. When we came to see her, she called Lecia by the wrong name. Then she came home, and it went to her brain, so she went crazy, and ants were crawling all over her arm. Then she died."

At the end of this report, Lecia and I would start scanning around whoever's kitchen it was for cookies or Kool-Aid. We knew with cer-tain instinct that reporting on a dead grandma deserved some pay-off. After a while, Lecia even learned to muster some tears, which could jack-up the ante as high as a Popsicle. (...) To this day, she claims that she genuinely mourned for the old lady, (...) and that I was too little and mean-spirited then to remember things right. I contend that her happy memories are shaped more by convenience than reality: she also recalls tatting as fun, and Ronald Reagan, for whom she voted twice, as a good guy. I couldn't have cried for Grandma under torture. But I knew my spiel and could nod earnestly to back up Lecia's snot-nosed snubbing.

The Liar's Club by Mary Karr

Memoir
F, 20+
Texas, 1961
Dramatic

*Mary Marlene reflects on the early years of her parents'
marriage.*

• • •

Sometime after New Year's, two bad things jump-started my parents
into an evil stretch—drinking and fighting. Mother blames Daddy
for this, and I suspect if Daddy had ever talked about such things,
he could have argued that it all started with Mother. It's one of
those chicken-and-egg problems. (...) I don't know who or what to
blame.

Nor can I figure what exactly led to Mother's near-fatal attack of
Nervous. Maybe drinking caused Mother to go crazy, or maybe the
craziness was just sort of standing in line to happen and the drinking actually staved it off a while. All I know is that first Mother was
drinking, then she and Daddy were fighting worse than ever, and
finally they were hauling her away in leather four-point restraints.

Drinking was not a totally new hobby in our house. Daddy always
drank, and with few ill effects that I can see. By *always,* I mean he
drank every day. He kept a six-pack in the fridge. Plus there was a
fifth of whiskey ratholed under the seat of his truck. (...) But drinking didn't change him much back then.(...)

Mother was another story. She had set down the drink when
Grandma came home to die, out of necessity, I guess. Then she
picked it up the night she got back from the funeral while we were
all rubbing on her. She'd said could I fetch her some Gallo wine and
7-UP from under the china cabinet (...) and I said sure. Then I
walked as slowly and miserably as any mule through any cotton row
in order to assemble that drink.

"The Life You Live (May Not Be Your Own)" by J. California Cooper

Short story
F, 40s
American South, Contemporary
Comic

After her husband leaves her for a younger woman, Molly finds a new freedom and confidence. Here she takes revenge on the women in her ladies club who had mocked her country ways.

• • •

In my reading class we had read Omar Khayyám, and I learned about wrapping food in grape leaves. At the last meeting before this one, I had served them, thinkin' it was some high-class stuff. I didn't know what to put in them, so I stuffed them with chitterlings. It was good to me! Viola had talked about me and laughed all over town. Made me look like a fool in front of everybody. Now you know why I wanted to pay her back. It's ugly, but it's true.

I let everybody in the club know the date for comin'. Then I went to try to find me some marijuana. It was hard to get! Didn't nobody know me that sells the stuff! But I finally got some. A quarter pound! When I prepared the food for that meetin', I mixed that stuff in everything I cooked. I put on a big pot of red beans. (...)

When them ladies, all dressed up so nice to show off, got to eatin' all my good food, they went to talkin' loud, laughin', and jumpin' all over the place, saying stupid things. Eatin' and drinkin' everything in sight! I had to snatch some things right off the trays and hurry up and replace 'em 'cause them ladies was gonna eat my dishes and furniture if I didn't! Dainty painted lips just guzzled the wine. (. . .) That marijuana must be something!

"The Life You Live (May Not Be Your Own)" by J. California Cooper

Short story
F, 40s
American South, Contemporary
Seriocomic

Molly finds that her husband of twenty-four years, Gravy, has been having an affair with a younger woman.

• • •

I'm tellin' you, I was hurt. Now, you hurt when somebody meets you and loves you up and in a few days you don't hear from them no more. But . . . this man been lovin' me up twenty-four years! (...) Well, that hurt filled my whole body and drug my heart down past my toes, and I had to drag it home, forcin' one foot at a time. Going home? Wasn't no home no more. Chile, I hurt! You hear me?

Now, I'm going to tell you somethin'. If you ain't ready to leave or lose your husband . . . don't get in his face and tell him nothin'! You wait till you got yourself together in your mind! You wait till you have made your heart understand . . . you can and will do without him! Otherwise, you may tell him you know what he's doin', thinking YOU smart and he's caught! And HE may say, "Well, since you know, now you know! I ain't giving her up!" Then what you gonna do?

Tell you what I did. (...) Gravy came home, sat in his favorite chair lookin' at TV, smokin' his pipe. I stared at him, waiting for him to see that I know. He didn't see me so I got up, put my hands on my fat hips, nose flaring wide open, and I told him I KNEW!

Gravy put his pipe down, just as calm as I ever seen him in my life, turned off the TV sat back down, put his hands on his knees, and told me . . . he wanted a divorce.

A DIVORCE?!

Little Women by Louisa May Alcott

Novel
F, 16
New England, circa 1875
Comic

As they sit together, sewing in the evening, Jo tells her sisters Beth, Meg, and Amy about her day.

• • •

I had a queer time with Aunt today, and as I got the best of it, I'll tell you about it (...). I was reading that everlasting Belsham, and droning away as I always do, for Aunt soon drops off and then I take out some nice book and read like fury till she wakes up. I actually made myself sleepy, and before she began to nod, I gave such a gape that she asked me what I meant by opening my mouth wide enough to take the whole book in at once.

I wish I could, and be done with it, (...)

Then she gave me a long lecture on my sins, and told me to sit and think them over while she just 'lost' herself for a moment. She never finds herself very soon, so the minute her cap began to bob like a top-heavy dahlia, I whipped *The Vicar of Wakefield* out of my pocket and read away, with one eye on him and one on Aunt. I'd just got to where they all tumbled into the water when I forgot, and laughed out loud. Aunt woke up, and being more good-natured after her nap, told me to read a bit, and show what frivolous work I preferred to the worthy and instructive Belsham. I did my best, and she liked it, though she only said: I don't understand what it's all about. Go back and begin it, child.

Back I went, and made the Primroses as interesting as ever I could. Once I was wicked enough to stop in a thrilling place and say meekly, "I'm afraid it tires you, ma'am. Shan't I stop now?"

Losing Isaiah by Seth J. Margolis

Novel
F, 20s
Contemporary Manhattan
Dramatic

*Selma, a young black woman, gives her lawyer the difficult
personal facts necessary in order to secure her son, whom
she has "sold" in an illegal adoption.*

• • •

I was a drug addict, and when Isaiah was born he was small. (...)

'Bout four weeks later the hospital called (...). I didn't think they'd
let me keep him. They were stupid to think that I could take care of
him. Least I managed to drag myself over there on the right day and
bring him home. At first I was almost happy. I'd sobered up for a
few hours and I kind of enjoyed just watching him sleeping. I
remember how his mouth would go like he was chewing, and the
way his eyes would roll around behind his lids. I was scared this
meant he was wanting crack. Now that I have experience with kids I
know they all chews and rolls their eyeballs when they sleep. Back
then, I thought my kid was addicted, on account of my taking drugs
early on. (...)

Things was okay until that night. I mean, I fed him and I changed
him and I thought maybe things was going to work out. But came
eleven or twelve at night and I needed to get out. You know what I
mean? I had to get *out*. And here was this infant needing watching
all the time. I'm thinking, Selma, what business you have with a
infant to care for? What made you think this was going to work
out? So I left him and went out. (...)

I shouldn'ta left him, but I did.

Love Medicine by Louise Erdrich

Novel
F, 60+
Minnesota, Ojibwe Reservation "rest home." Contemporary
Seriocomic

Lulu, now blind, serene but adamant, describes her youth.

• • •

No one ever understood my wild and secret ways. They used to say Lulu Lamartine was like a cat, loving no one, only purring to get what she wanted. But that's not true. I was in love with the whole world and all that lived in its rainy arms. Sometimes I'd look out on my yard and the green leaves would be glowing. I'd see the oil slick on the wing of a grackle. I'd hear the wind rushing, rolling, like the far-off sound of waterfalls. Then I'd open my mouth wide, my ears wide, my heart, and I'd let everything inside.

After some time I'd swing my door shut and walk back into the house with my eyes closed. I'd sit there like that in my house. I'd sit there with my eyes closed on beauty until it was time to make the pickle brine or smash the boiled berries or the boys came home. But for a while after letting the world in I would be full. I wouldn't want anything more but what I had.

And so when they tell you that I was heartless, a shameless man-chaser, don't ever forget this: I loved what I saw. And yes, it is true that I've done all the things they say. That's not what gets them. What aggravates them is I've never shed one solitary tear. I'm not sorry. That's unnatural. As we all know, a woman is supposed to cry.

Mariette in Ecstasy by Ron Hansen

Novel
F, 17
Our Lady of Sorrows, Church and Priory of the Sisters of the
  Crucifixion, upstate New York, 1906
Dramatic

*Mariette Baptiste, postulant Bride of Christ, has been
blessed—or cursed—with stigmata, or "stigmatized."*

• • •

I have been told to receive our hundreds of Sunday visitors in the
parlor, but all who speak to me think I am insane. My head empties
and I do not know how to reply to them. Surely Mother Superior
must be demented to think me fit for such duties. I hold no conver-
sations but those I have with you. I have no interest in people unless
I see Jesus in them.

Mother Saint-Raphael has forbidden me Communion for six days
now. Oh, how I ache for him, and how tortured and sick and deso-
late I have felt without him! I grieve to imagine how dull and hag-
gard and ugly his Mariette must seem to him now! And yet I should
think myself hateful if being deprived of him for these six days had
not grossly disfigured me.

What a cruel mistress I am to complain so much about your absence
when I should be wooing you and praising you for your kindnesses
and sweet presence. You see, though, that I have become obsessed
by you. You are not here with me enough if for one brief moment I
have no sense of you. And yet I have only gratitude for the despera-
tion you have caused me, and I loathe the peace in which I lived
before I truly knew you.

Mariette in Ecstasy by Ron Hansen

Novel
F, Teen–20s
A convent, upstate New York, 1906
Dramatic

Mariette, a postulate nun, swoons as she describes the state under which she receives the miracle of the stigmata.

• • •

In prayer I float out of myself. I seek God with a great yearning (...). I have lost my body; I don't know where I am or even if I am now human or spirit. A sweet power is drawing me (...), effortless but insistent. I flush with excitement and a balm of tenderness seems to flow over me. And when I have gotten to a fullness of joy and peace and tranquillity, then I know I have been possessed by Jesus and have completely lost myself in him. Oh, what a blissful abandonment it is! Everything in my being tells me to stay there. Every thought I have is of his infinite perfection. Every feeling I have is of his kindness and heavenly love (...). Hours may pass, but I have no sense of tiredness or pain or needs of any kind (...). I have no use for speech except to praise him. I have no desires except to be held there by him forever. I have a vision of him but I cannot see his face or his form, only infinite light and goodness. I hear his voice in an interior way, his words have sweetness and charm but no sound, and yet they are more felt and permanent in my soul than if I heard Jesus pronounce them (...). And then such a great sorrow for my sins takes possession of me and it seems to me I would rather die a horrible death than ever sin against God again.

"The Member of the Wedding" by Carson McCullers

Short story
F, 30s–40s
The south, 1930s
Dramatic

Berenice, the African-American cook, tries to prevent twelve-year-old Frankie from acting on her misconceived fantasy.

• • •

I see what you have in your mind. Don't think I don't. You see something unheard of at Winter Hill tomorrow, and you right in the center. You think you going to march down the center of the aisle right in between your brother and the bride. You think you going to break into that wedding, and Jesus knows what else. (...)

I see through them eyes. Don't argue with me. (...)

But what I'm warning is this (...). If you start out falling in love with some unheard-of-thing like that, what is going to happen to you? If you take a mania like this, it won't be the last time and of that you can be sure. So what will become of you? Will you be trying to break into weddings the rest of your days? And what kind of life would that be? (...) You just laying yourself this fancy trap to catch yourself in trouble (...). And you know it.

"The Member of the Wedding" by Carson McCullers

Short story
F, 12
The south, 1930s
Seriocomic

*Frankie, a girl with an intense desire to belong, childishly
believes she will accompany her brother and his bride on
their honeymoon.*

• • •

Boyoman! Manoboy! When we leave Winter Hill we're going to
more places than you ever thought about or even knew existed. Just
where we will go first I don't know, and it don't matter. Because
after we go to that place we're going on to another. We mean to
keep moving, the three of us. Here today and gone tomorrow.
Alaska, China, Iceland, South America. Traveling on trains. Letting
her rip on motorcycles. Flying around all over the world in aero-
planes. Here today and gone tomorrow. All over the world. It's the
damn truth. Boyoman! (...)

And we will meet them. Everybody. We will just walk up to people
and know them right away. We will be walking down a dark road
and see a lighted house and knock on the door and strangers will
rush to meet us and say: Come in! Come in! We will know decorated
aviators and New York people and movie stars. We will have thousands of friends, thousands and thousands and thousands of
friends. We will belong to so many clubs that we can't even keep
track of all of them. We will be members of the whole world.
Boyoman! Manoboy!

"The Member of the Wedding"
by Carson McCullers

Short story
F, 30s–40s
The south, 1930s
Dramatic

Berenice, the African-American cook for Frankie and her family, tells how she came to marry again after her first husband, Ludie, died.

• • •

To understand this, you have to know what happened after Ludie died (...). I won't go into the whole business, but what happened was that I was cheated by them policy people out of fifty dollars. And in two days I had to scour around and raise the fifty dollars to make out for the funeral. Because I couldn't let Ludie be put away cheap. I pawned everything I could lay hands on. And I sold my coat and Ludie's coat. To that second-hand clothing store on Front Avenue. (...)

I was walking down that street alongside of the City Hall one evening when I suddenly seen this shape before me. Now the shape of this boy ahead of me was so similar to Ludie through the shoulders and the back of the head that I almost dropped dead there on the sidewalk. I followed and ran behind him. It was Henry Johnson, and that was the first time I ever saw him also, since he lived in the country and didn't come much into town. But he had chanced to buy Ludie's coat and he was built on the same shape as Ludie. And from the back view it looked like he was Ludie's ghost or Ludie's twin. But how I married him I don't exactly know, for to begin with it was clear that he did not have his share of sense. But you let a boy hang around and you get fond of him. Anyway, that's how I married Henry Johnson.

"The Metamorphosis" by Franz Kafka

Short story
F, Late teens, early 20s
1915, a city
Dramatic

Grete implores her parents to put out the hideous, insect-like creature into which her brother has seemingly transformed.

• • •

My dear parents, things can't go on like this. Perhaps you don't realise that, but I do. I won't utter my brother's name in the presence of this creature, and so all I say is: we must try to get rid of it. We've tried to look after it and to put up with it as far as is humanly possible, and I don't think anyone could reproach us in the slightest. (...)

... it will be the death of both of you, I can see that coming. When one has to work as hard as we do, all of us, one can't stand this continual torment at home on top of it. At least I can't stand it any longer. *(She sobs...)*

He must go, (...) that's the only solution, Father. You must try to get rid of the idea that this is Gregor. The fact that we've believed it for so long is the root of all our trouble. But how can it be Gregor? If this were Gregor, he would have realized long ago that human beings can't live with such a creature, and he'd have gone away of this own accord. Then we wouldn't have any brother, but we'd be able to go on living and keep his memory in honour. As it is, this creature persecutes us, drives away our lodgers, obviously wants the whole apartment to himself and would have us all sleep in the gutter. Just look, Father, (...) he's at it again!

"Missionaries" from *How I Came West and Why I Stayed* by Alison Baker

Short story
F, 17
A small town in the western United States. Contemporary
Comic

*Willa's older sister, Elaine, is having an affair with Willa's
gymnastics coach. Willa disapproves.*

• • •

Sometimes I drive past Elaine's apartment. Sometimes I park on the
street and sit in the car, looking up at her windows. She's fastidious
about closing the curtains, but I know when she's not alone. I can
see Elaine and Coach together, Coach taking off his striped shirt,
unfastening his black leather belt, letting his pants drop to the floor.
Elaine letting her bathrobe fall beside them.

Coach was an athlete. He's still a vigorous man. I can see him picking her up off the floor, lifting her in his arms, arranging her the
way he wants her. He has thick, muscular legs, and sometimes he
stands over her, lifting weights, jumping up and grabbing onto the
light fixture, chinning himself as she watches from below. He drops
to the floor and does a dozen push-ups, then rolls into a headstand.
Elaine can't move. Coach raises himself onto his hands and walks
on them over to the bed.

I know when Coach is there, because he parks his car in the street. I
park behind it. Elaine is something like a slug, I think; a large pink
slug that lies inert, waiting to have something done to it.

I do things to his car. (...) I scoop up a lot of rotting leaves from the
gutter and paste them on his windshield. The next time, I bring a
bar of Dial that I took from Jenny's locker when she was in the
shower and write COACH on the windshield. GOD WAS HERE. I
write backwards, on the back window, so he can read it (...) as he
drives away.

"Modern Love" from *If the River Was Whiskey* by Coraghessan T. Boyle

Short story
F, 20s/30s
Contemporary
Comic

On their second date, Breda makes a confession to her partner.

• • •

I can't tell you what a strain it was for me the other night (...). I mean the Thai food, the seats in the movie theater, the ladies room in that place for god's sake (...). Have you seen the Health Department statistics on sanitary conditions in ethnic restaurants? (...)

These people are refugees. They have—well, different standards. They haven't even been inoculated (...). The illegals, anyway. And that's half of them (...). I got drunk from fear (...). Blind panic. I couldn't help thinking I'd wind up with hepatitis or dysentery or dengue fever or something (...).

I usually bring a disposable sanitary sheet for public theaters—just think of who might have been in that seat before you, and how many times, and what sort of nasty festering little cultures of this and that there must be in all those ancient dribbles of taffy and Coke and extra-butter popcorn—but I didn't want you to think I was too extreme or anything on the first date, so I didn't. And the ladies' room(...) You don't think I'm overreacting, do you?

Montana 1948 by Larry Watson

Novel
F, 30s
Montana, 1948
Dramatic

Gail tries to convince her husband, a sheriff, that his brother Frank, a doctor, should be arrested.

• • •

The reason, Wesley, the reason Marie didn't want to be examined by Frank is that he—he has (...) is that your brother has molested Indian girls. (...)

No, wait. Listen to me, please. Marie said she didn't want to be alone with him. You should have seen her. She was practically hysterical about having me stay in the room. And once Frank left she told me all of it. He's been doing it for years, Wes. When he examines an Indian he...he does things he shouldn't. He takes liberties. Indecent liberties. *(...)*

What things? I'll tell you what things. Your brother makes his patients—*some* of his patients—undress completely and get into indecent positions. He makes them jump up and down while he watches. He fondles their breasts. He—no, don't you turn away. *Don't!* You asked and I'm going to tell you. All of it. He puts things into these girls. Inside them, *there*. His instruments. His fingers. He has...your brother I believe has inserted his, his penis into some of these girls. Wesley, your brother is raping these women. These *girls*. These Indian girls. He offers his services to the reservation, to the BIA school. To the high school for athletic physicals. Then when he gets these girls where he wants them (...). *Oh!* I don't even want to say it again. *He does what he wants to do.*

"Mrs. Darcy Meets the Blue-Eyed Stranger at the Beach" from *Cakew* by Lee Smith

Short story
F, 20s
Contemporary South
Comic

Ginny complains to her sisters about their mother.

• • •

You know what really drove me mad? (...) I was telling my shrink this the other day. I mean, whenever I think of Mama, you know what I think of her doing? I think of her putting leftovers in a smaller container. Like, say, we've had a roast, right? And if it were *me*, I'd leave the roast in the pan it was in. But oh no. After dinner, she had to find a smaller pan, right? For the refrigerator. Tupperware, or something. The Tupperware post-roast container. Then somebody makes a sandwich maybe, and one inch of the roast is gone, so she had to find another container. Then another, then another, then another. She must have gone through about fifteen containers for every major thing she fixed. That's all I can remember of childhood.

"My Diagnosis" from *Girl, Interrupted* by Susanna Kaysen

Memoir
F, 20+
Contemporary
Dramatic

With mild trepidation, a former mental patient questions "illness" and "recovery."

• • •

I got better and Daisy didn't and I can't explain why. Maybe I was just flirting with madness the way I flirted with my teachers and my classmates. I wasn't convinced I was crazy, though I feared I was. Some people say that having any conscious opinion on the matter is a mark of sanity, but I'm not sure that's true. I still think about it. I'll always have to think about it.

I often ask myself if I'm crazy. I ask other people too.

"Is this a crazy thing to say?" (...)

I start a lot of sentences with "Maybe I'm totally nuts," or "Maybe I've gone 'round the bend."

If I do something out of the ordinary—take two baths in one day, for example—I say to myself: Are you crazy?

It's a common phrase, I know. But it means something particular to me: the tunnels, the security screens, the plastic forks, the shimmering, ever-shifting borderline that like all boundaries beckons and asks to be crossed. I do not want to cross it again.

"My Father's Daughter" from *Personals* by Bliss Broyard

Essay
F, 30+
Contemporary
Seriocomic

A woman tells how she enjoys the company of her father's friends.

• • •

There is a particular type of older man I like. He must be at least twenty years my senior, preferably thirty years or more. Old enough to be my father, it's fair to say. This man is handsome, stylish, a connoisseur of women, intelligent, cultured and witty, old-fashioned and romantic. He has male friends whom he loves as brothers. He knows how to dance the old dances: the lindy, the cha-cha, the samba, even the tango. He's vain about his appearance and is unabashedly delighted any time I tell him he is looking trim or healthy or particularly handsome. When I compliment his fedora, he tilts it to an even more jaunty angle. He reads the romantic poets and can quote their lines in a way that doesn't sound corny. (...) He tells me stories about girls he knew overseas: geishas and lonely nurses. He notices what I am wearing; he notices if I have changed my hair style or done my makeup in a new way. Each time I see him, he tells me I've never looked better. (...) Many of the traits in my favorite type of older man I would find foolish, affected, or tiresome in a younger man, but with you, old sport, I am always charmed.

"The Ocean" from *Shiloh and Other Stories* by Bobbie Ann Mason

Short story
F, 60+
The South, 1970s
Seriocomic

While watching TV in their camper, Imogene suddenly goes off on her husband, Bill. She is crying.

• • •

Years ago (...) when I took your mama to the doctor—when she had just moved in with us and I took her for a checkup?—I went in to talk to the doctor and he said to me, 'How are *you*?' and I said, 'I didn't come to see the doctor, I brought *her*,' and he said, 'I know, but how are *you*?' He said to me, 'She'll kill you! I've seen it before, and she'll kill you. You think they won't be much trouble and it's best, but mark my words, you may not see it now, but she'll take it out of you. She could destroy you. You could end up being a wreck.' (...)

She was your mama (...). And I'm the one that took care of her all that time, keeping her house, putting up her canning, putting out her wash, and then waiting on her when she got down. And you never lifted a finger. You couldn't be around old people, you said; it gives you the heebie-jeebies. Well, listen, buster, your time's a-coming and who's going to wait on you? You can stick me in a rest home, for all I care. And another thing, you don't see Miz Lillian living at the White House.

The Odyssey by Homer

Epic poem
F, 40+
Ancient Greece, 11th Century B.C.
Dramatic

*Penelope's nurse, Eurycleia, entreats Penelope to come
down from her room to witness her husband's dramatic
homecoming.*

• • •

Wake,
wake up, dear child! Penelope, come down,
see with your own eyes what all these years you longed for!
Odysseus is here! Oh, in the end, he came!
And he has killed your suitors, killed them all
who made his house a bordello and ate his cattle
and raised their hands against his son! (...)

I did not see it,
I knew nothing; only I heard the groans
of men dying. We sat still in the inner rooms
holding our breath, and marveling, shut in,
until Telemakhos came to the door and called me—
your own dear son, sent this time by his father!
So I went out, and found Odysseus
erect, with dead men littering the floor
this way and that. If you had only seen him!
It would have made you heart glow hot!—a lion
splashed with mire and blood.

But now the cold
corpses are all-gathered at the gate,
and he has cleansed his hall with fire and brimstone,
a great blaze. Then he sent me here to you.
Come with me: you may both embark this time
for happiness together, after pain,

after long years. Here is your prayer, your passion,
granted: your own lord lives, he is at home,
he found you safe, he found his. The suitors
abused his house, but he has brought them down.

"On Being a Cripple" from *Plaintext* by Nancy Mairs

Essay
F, 30+
1986
Seriocomic

A woman, a writer with multiple sclerosis, castigates euphemism.

• • •

First, the matter of semantics. I am a cripple. I choose this word to name me. I choose from among several possibilities, the most common of which are "handicapped" and "disabled." I made the choice a number of years ago, without thinking, unaware of my motives for doing so. (...) People—crippled or not—wince at the word "cripple," as they do not at "handicapped" or "disabled." Perhaps I want them to wince. I want them to see me as a tough customer, one to whom the fates/god/viruses have not been kind, but who can face the brutal truth of her existence squarely. As a cripple, I swagger.

But, to be fair to myself, a certain amount of honesty underlies my choice. "Cripple" seems to me a clean word, straighforward and precise. It has an honorable history, having made its first appearance in the Lindisfarne Gospel in the tenth century. As a lover of words, I like the accuracy with which it describes my condition: I have lost the full use of my limbs. "Disabled" by contrast, suggests any incapacity, physical or mental. And I certainly don't like "handicapped," which implies that I have deliberately been put at a disadvantage, by whom I can't imagine (my God is not my Handicapper General), in order to equalize chances in the great race of life. These words seem to me to be moving away from my condition, to be widening the gap between word and reality. Most remote is the recently coined euphemism "differently abled," which partakes of the same semantic hopefulness that transformed countries from "undeveloped" to "underdeveloped," then to "less developed," and finally to "developing" nations. People have continued to starve in those countries during the shift.

"People Like That Are the Only People Here" by Lorrie Moore

Short story
F, 30s/40s
Contemporary
Seriocomic

The opening paragraphs of a new mother's story—

• • •

A BEGINNING, an end: there seems to be neither. The whole thing is like a cloud that just lands, and everywhere inside it is full of rain. A start: the Mother finds a blood clot in the Baby's diaper. What is the story? Who put this here? It is big and bright, with a broken, khaki-colored vein in it. Over the weekend, the Baby had looked listless and spacy, clayey and grim. But today he looks fine—so what is this thing, startling against the white diaper, like a tiny mouse heart packed in snow? Perhaps it belongs to someone else. Perhaps it is something menstrual, something belonging to the Mother or to the Babysitter, something the Baby has found in a wastebasket and for his own demented baby reasons stowed away here. (Babies— they're crazy! What can you do?) In her mind, the Mother takes this away from his body and attaches it to someone else's. There. Doesn't that make more sense?

Still, she phones the children's hospital clinic. Blood in the diaper, she says, and sounding alarmed and perplexed, the woman on the other end says, "Come in now."

Such pleasingly instant service! Just say "blood." Just say "diaper." Look what you get.

Ragtime by E.L. Doctorow

Novel
F, 40+
New York, 1902
Dramatic

Emma Goldman, anarchist orator and agitator, speaks in the Workingmen's Hall on East 14th Street.

• • •

Love in freedom! Those who (...) have paid with blood and tears for their spiritual awakening, repudiate marriage as an imposition, a shallow empty mockery. (...)

Comrades and brothers, (...) can you socialists ignore the double bondage of one-half of the human race? Do you think the society that plunders your labor has no interest in the way you are asked to live with women? Not through freedom but through bondage? All the reformers talk today of the white slavery problem. But if white slavery is a problem, why is marriage not a problem? Is there no connection between the institution of marriage and the institution of the brothel? (...)

The truth is, (...) women may not vote, they may not love whom they want, they may not develop their minds and their spirits, they may not commit their lives to the spiritual adventure of life, comrades they may not! And why? Is our genius only in our wombs? Can we not write books and create learned scholarship and perform music and provide philosophical models for the betterment of mankind? Must our fate always be physical?

Ragtime by E.L. Doctorow

Novel
F, 40+
New York, 1902
Dramatic

Emma Goldman counsels Younger Brother, who is grieving the departure of a lover he has stalked and briefly won.

• • •

I don't know where she is. But if I could tell you, what good would that do? Suppose you got her to come back to you? She would only stay awhile. She would run away from you again, don't you know that? (...) You look terrible, (...) What have you been doing to yourself? Don't you eat? Don't you get any fresh air? (...) You have aged ten years. I cannot sympathize. You think you are special, losing your lover. It happens every day. Suppose she consented to live with you after all. You're a bourgeois, you would want to marry her. You would destroy each other inside of a year. You would see her begin to turn old and bored under your very eyes. You would sit across the dinner table from each other in bondage, in terrible bondage to what you thought was love. The both of you. Believe me you are better off this way. (...)This way you can feel sorry for yourself. (...) And what a delicious emotion that is. I'll tell you something. In this room tonight you saw my present lover but also two of my former lovers. We are all good friends. Friendship is what endures. Shared ideals, respect for the whole character of a human being. Why can't you accept your own freedom? Why do you have to cling to someone in order to live?

Rambling Rose by Calder Willingham

Novel
F, 19
Deep South, 1935
Seriocomic

Rose, from Birmingham, Alabama, was hired as live-in help by Buddy's father. Deeply ashamed of her easily aroused sexual feelings, she apologizes to Buddy (age thirteen) for the heavy petting that occurred between them the night before.

• • •

Buddy, I didn't mean to come back, I didn't, but I have to ask you, as bad as I've been please have pity on me and don't ruin me by telling them what I did (...). I didn't really mean you no harm, I'd never want to hurt a hair on your head and that's the truth, I love you, I wouldn't want to hurt you ever. But everybody would think I did, they'd think I was an awful girl, they'd despise me and hate me (...).

Buddy, please don't tell them. Please don't. I can't get no other job—and that ain't even the most important thing, but I can't. I really can't, Buddy, it's a depression goin' on, they ain't no jobs. I know cause I looked and looked and couldn't find nothin', nothin;' at all. Now I ain't just trying' to make you feel sorry for me, but I weared out my shoes looking' for some work, Buddy, I was hungry, real hungry, and I didn't have no place to stay, but I couldn't find no job nowheres because there just wasn't none. All I could of done was to be, to be a...well, you wouldn't know about it, but I couldn't do that, never, I couldn't (...). There wasn't nothin' I could do, till your Daddy helped me and gimme this place, which saved my life in more ways than you could know (...).

Buddy, if you like me even a little bit, please don't tell them (...). Buddy I know I'm no good, I'm a bad girl but I can't help it, please have pity on me and don't tell! Please don't tell, please don't (...).

Rambling Rose by Calder Willingham

Novel
F, 19
Deep South, 1935
Seriocomic

Rose, an "oversexed" young woman from Birmingham, Alabama, has met Mr. Right at last.

• • •

First, he never got tired of listenin' to me. I talk an awful lot and sometimes men get tired of it and tell me to shut up. Twice I ast him if he minded me talkin' so much and he says no, he loved to hear me talk. That's what he said, Buddy, them were his very words! But more than that, in all them hours, Buddy, do you know what? The only thing he ever done was hold my hand, now how about that? He didn't even try to kiss me! All he done was hold my hand while we sat and talked, that's all! He didn't even kiss me when he took me home, and he'd spent all day with me and bought me a T-bone steak that cost him a lotta money! He shook *hands* with me, that's what he did, and he says, 'Thank you for a wonderful evenin'. Can I see you in the mornin', it is my day off'—he loves me, he loves me, Buddy! This is the happiest day of my life, he is comin' here tomorrow mornin' at nine and I bet before the day is over he asks me to marry him! And don't you know I'll sure say yes! I have met Mr. Right at last, Buddy, I have met him at last!

The Rapture of Canaan
by Sheri Reynolds

Novel
F, 15
Contemporary South
Dramatic

Ninah, granddaughter of "the founder of the church of Fire and Brimstone and God's Almighty Baptizing Wind," an isolated sect ruled by its patriarch, is pregnant, at 14, by her "prayer partner," James.

• • •

Some people say you can't change history, but that isn't entirely true. We did it at Fire and Brimstone, and it was easy.

James didn't take his own life. He drowned on a hot night, caught on a root in the bottom of the pond. Nobody ever mentioned that he was tethered to that sunken tree with thick, deliberate knots.

And that was that. At his funeral, with everybody crying and howling so, nobody even blinked when Grandpa Herman said his death was accidental. Nobody minded that he praised James and talked about what a good companion he'd make for the angels. That's what we wanted to hear.

Pammy couldn't stop shaking. She shook for the rest of that summer, and the only thing that made her stop was sitting between my legs and letting me practice on her hair. I learned French braiding after James died. I worked on Pammy's red hair until it looked like something out of magazine, and even though in the past the adults wouldn't have let us wear our hair in fancy braids, nobody seemed to notice or care. (...)

I went into James' bedroom right afterwards and sifted through his drawers without asking. I took one of his flannel shirts and wore it all the time, even though it was still summer. When I buttoned it over my dress, it bagged down like my heart, and I liked the way it looked and wouldn't take it off.

"Roman Fever" from *Roman Fever and Other Stories* by Edith Wharton

Short story
F, 50s
Rome, 1930
Seriocomic

Mrs. Slade reveals a long-kept secret to her old friend, Mrs. Ansley. Both are widows, in Rome again after many years with their respective daughters.

• • •

You think I'm bluffing, don't you? Well, you went to meet the man I was engaged to—and I can repeat every word of the letter that took you there. (...)

Listen, if you don't believe me. 'My one darling, things can't go on like this. I must see you alone. Come to the Colosseum immediately after dark tomorrow. There will be somebody to let you in. No one whom you need fear will suspect'—but perhaps you've forgotten what the letter said? (...)

And if you burnt the letter you're wondering how on earth I know what was in it. That's it, isn't it? (...)

Well, my dear, I know what was in that letter because I wrote it! (...)

Yes; I wrote it! But I was the girl he was engaged to. Did you happen to remember that? (...) And still you went? (...)

I'd found out—and I hated you, hated you. I knew you were in love with Delphin—and I was afraid; afraid of you, of your quiet ways, your sweetness...your...well, I wanted you out of the way, that's all. Just for a few weeks; just till I was sure of him. So in a blind fury I wrote that letter...I don't know why I'm telling you now. (...)

I wish now I hadn't told you. I'd no idea you'd feel about it as you do; I thought you'd be amused. It all happened so long ago, as you say; and you must do me the justice to remember that I had no reason to think you'd ever taken it seriously. How could I, when you were married to Horace Ansley two months afterward? (...) People were rather surprised—they wondered at its being done so quickly; but I thought I knew. I had an idea you did it out of pique—to be able to say you'd got ahead of Delphin and me. Girls have such silly reasons for doing the most serious things. And your marrying so soon convinced me that you'd never really cared. (...)

I suppose I did it as a sort of joke— (...)

Delphin there? They let you in? Oh—now you're lying! (...)

Came? How did he know he'd find you? (...)

Oh, God—you answered! I never thought of your answering.

"The Same Old Story"
by Andrea Freud Loewenstein

Short story
F, 30s/40s
Contemporary
Seriocomic

A woman laments her lover's lack of response.

• • •

It's the same old story. I loved her. She didn't love me back.

Or maybe she did love me back at first, a little, but not enough to get in her car and come over that time we were talking on the phone and she said you keep saying you have to talk, well go on I'm listening, and I said I can't not with you sounding like that, and she said I feel like this is about nothing it's just air and I don't want to do it and so I'm getting off the phone now, and I didn't say anything because I was crying and she said in a begrudging sort of voice I'm sorry if I hurt you, and we hung up.

And I sat at the window grading my exams and crying and waiting a little hopefully for her to drive up in her small blue very clean car, because she kept her car as clean as the day she bought it, and get out of her car and come up my steps and into the room and take me in her arms. She could have left after that, dayenu as they say, it would have been enough, I had abandoned other kinds of hopes a long time ago. I didn't need her to say anything. Not I won't go to bed with you but I still love you. Not here I am and I'll stay as long as you want me, it won't kill me to get to bed late for once in my life. Nothing.

"The Search" from *Where the Sidewalk Ends* by Shel Silverstein

Poem
F/M, child
Contemporary
Seriocomic

The speaker seeks an exploration.

• • •

I went to find the pot of gold
That's waiting where the rainbow ends.
I searched and searched and searched and searched
And searched and searched, and then—
There it was, deep in the grass,
Under an old and twisty bough.
It's mine, it's mine, it's mine at last...
What do I search for now?

"Saul and Patsy Are Pregnant" from *A Relative Stranger* by Charles Baxter

Short story
F, 20s/30s
Contemporary
Seriocomic

Patsy tells her husband, Saul, what she wants, what she likes.

• • •

I want a motorcycle, I've been thinking about it. We don't need another car, but I want a motorcycle. I always have. Women *can* ride motorcycles, Saul, don't deny it. Oh. And another thing (...) This morning I was trying to think of where the Cayuse Indians lived, and I couldn't remember, and we don't have an encyclopedia to check. We need that. (...)

Saul, why are you looking like that? Are you in a state? (...) You *are* in a state. (...) What is it this time? Our recent brush with death? The McPhees? (…)

[T]hey were so cute, the two of them. So sweet. And so young, too. And I know you, Saul, and I know what you thought. You thought: what have these two got that I don't have? (…)

[Y]ou can't be like them because you can't, Saul. You fret. That's your hobby. It's how you stay occupied. You've heard about spots? About how a person can't change them? Well, I *like* your spots. I like how you're a professional worrier. And you always know about things like the Cayuse Indians, I'm not like that. And I don't want to be married to somebody like me. I'd put myself to sleep. But you're perfect. You're an early warning system. You bark and growl at life. You're my dog. You do see that, don't you?

"See Also" from *The Giant's House* by Elizabeth McCracken

Novel
F, 50+
New England, contemporary
Seriocomic

Peggy is bemused.

• • •

I do not love mankind.

People think they're interesting. That's their first mistake. Every retiree you meet wants to supply you with his life story. (...) A life story can make adequate conversation but bad history.

Still, there you are in a nursing home, bored and lonely, and one day something different happens. Instead of a gang of school kids come to bellow Christmas carols at you, there's this earnest young person with a tape recorder, wanting to know about a flood sixty years ago, or what Main Street was like, or some such nonsense. All the other people in the home are sick to death of hearing your stories, because really let's be honest you only have a few.

Suddenly there's a microphone in your face. Wham! just like that, you're no longer a dull conversationalist, you're a natural resource.

The Silence of the Lambs
by Thomas Harris

Novel
F, 30s
Contemporary Baltimore
Dramatic

*Clarice Starling is manipulated into revealing significant inci-
dents in her childhood by Dr. Hannibal Lechter, a brilliant
psychologist and grisly killer.*

• • •

I found something strange in the barn. They had a little tack room
out there. I thought this thing was some kind of old helmet. When I
got it down, it was stamped "W. W. Greener's Humane Horse
Killer." (...) They were going to kill [my horse] (...). I worried about it
all the time. She was getting pretty fat. (...)

Early. Still dark(...). I woke up and heard the lambs screaming. I
woke up in the dark and the lambs were screaming (...). I couldn't
do anything for them. I was just a— (...)

I got dressed without turning on the light and went outside. She
was scared. All the horses in the pen were scared and milling
around. I blew in her nose and she knew it was me. Finally she'd
put her nose in my hand. The lights were on in the barn and in the
shed by the sheep pen. Bare bulbs, big shadows. The refrigerator
truck had come and it was idling, roaring. I led her away.

"Silent Dancing" from *Silent Dancing: A Partial Remembrance of a Puerto Rican Childhood* by Judith Ortiz Cofer

Novel
F, 17
Puerto Rico, 1960s
Dramatic

At a neighborhood party, a Puerto Rican woman vows to become "American." (Humilde refers to the way a young woman was supposed to act: expressing humility in all her actions.)

• • •

I do what I want. This is not some primitive island I live on. Do they expect me to wear a black mantilla on my head and go to mass every day? Not me. I'm an American woman and I will do as I please. I can type faster than anyone in my senior class at Central High, and I'm going to be a secretary to a lawyer when I graduate. I can pass for an American girl anywhere—I've tried it—at least for Italian, anyway. I never speak Spanish in public. I hate these parties, but I wanted the dress. I look better than any of these humildes here. My life is going to be different. I have an American boyfriend. He is older and has a car. My parents don't know it, but I sneak out of the house late at night sometimes to be with him. If I marry him, even my name will be American. I hate rice and beans. It's what makes these women fat.

Snow Falling on Cedars
by David Guterson

Novel
F, 40s
Puget Sound, 1954
Dramatic

Fujiko, a Japanese woman, tries to ward off the pain her teenage daughter, Hatsue, will someday endure as a result of falling in love with a white boy.

• • •

I could say (…) that living among the *hajukin* has tainted you, made your soul impure, Hatsue. This lack of purity envelops you—I see it every day. You carry it with you always. It is like a mist around your soul, and it haunts your face like a shadow at moments when you do not protect it well. I see it in your eagerness to leave here and walk in the woods in the afternoon. I cannot translate all of this easily, except as the impurity that comes with living each day among the white people. I am not asking you to shun them entirely—this you should not do. You must live in this world, of course you must, and this world is the world of the *hajukin*—you must learn to live in it, you must go to school. But don't allow *living among the hajukin* to become living *intertwined* with them. Your soul will decay. Something fundamental will rot and go sour. You are eighteen, you are grown now—I can't walk with you where you are going any-more. You walk alone soon, Hatsue. I hope you will carry your purity with you always and remember the truth of who you are.

The Sweet Hereafter by Russell Banks

Novel
F, 20s
Contemporary
Dramatic

*In an attempt to hurt her father beyond healing, Zoe calls
him from a pay phone to taunt him with the self-destructive
choices she's made.*

• • •

You mean, Daddy, am I *stoned*? Do I have a *needle* dangling from
my arm? Am I nodding in a phone booth? Did I *score* this morning,
get whacked, Daddy, and call you for *money*? (...)

God...I don't fucking *believe* it (...). I'm calling (...) because I have
some news for you. Daddy, I've got some big news for you. (...)

Okay. Okay, then. You won't want to hear this, but I'm gonna say it
anyhow. Dig it. I went to sell blood yesterday. That's how it is. I'm in
fucking New York City, where my father is a hot shit lawyer, and I'm
selling my blood for thirty-five bucks. (...)

They wouldn't take my blood (...). I tested HIV positive(...) You know
what that means, Daddy? Do you? Does it register? (...) AIDS,
Daddy. (...)

Welcome to hard times, Daddy (...). Isn't that a kick, Daddy? (...)

What do I want you to do? [She practically shrieked it. Then she
laughed, a long high-pitched cackle, like an old madwoman, a
witch on the heath.] (...)

Money (...). I want money. (...)

I can hear you breathing, Daddy. (...)

Give me a thousand bucks. For now (...). That's all I've got, Daddy.
All I've got is now. Remember? AIDS, Daddy. (...)

I love you, Daddy. Oh, God, I'm scared.

Talk before Sleep by Elizabeth Berg

Novel
F, 42
Contemporary
Dramatic

Ruth is dying of cancer. She is talking to her best friend.

• • •

You know, I never thought dying would be boring. Did you? I mean,
I find myself getting to this place of readiness. It's a kind of deep
peace, that I never felt before. And so I lie there thinking, okay, I
guess this is it, this is a good time, go ahead; and then the phone
rings and it's somebody wanting to steam clean my wall-to-wall car-
peting, which of course I don't even have. And I want to say, 'Oh,
stop with this carpet nonsense. Listen to me. You've got to be care-
ful. Say all you need to say, right away. You have no idea how frag-
ile this all is!' But of course all I say is 'No thank you.' (...)

And you know what else? It's such a rich thing. It's so good. And
sometimes I think, God, my life has taken these awful turns, but
they're also sort of wonderful. I mean, the constant presence of you
all—my friends (...). Sometimes I feel as if I want to stay sick so I can
keep all this (...).

I don't want to die, but sometimes I wonder (...). Wouldn't it be terribly anticlimactic if I went back to normal? I mean, for all of us?

"A Telephone Call" from *The Portable Dorothy Parker* by Dorothy Parker

Short story
F, 20+
1930s
Comic

A woman waits anxiously by the phone for a man to call.

• • •

This is the last time I'll look at the clock. I will not look at it again. It's ten minutes past seven. He said he would telephone at five o'clock. "I'll call you at five, darling." I think that's where he said "darling." I'm almost sure he said it there. I know he called me "darling" twice, and the other time was when he said good-by. "Good-by, darling." He was busy, and he can't say much in the office, but he called me "darling" twice. He couldn't have minded my calling him up. I know you shouldn't keep telephoning them—I know they don't like that. When you do that, they know you are thinking about them and wanting them, and that makes them hate you. But I hadn't talked to him in three days—not in three days. And all I did was ask him how he was; it was just the way anybody might have called him up. He couldn't have minded that. He couldn't have thought I was bothering him. "No, of course you're not," he said. And he said he'd telephone me. He didn't have to say that. I didn't ask him to, truly I didn't. I'm sure I didn't. I don't think he would say he'd telephone me, and then just never do it. Please don't let him do that, God. Please don't.

"I'll call you at five darling." "Good-by, darling."

Tending to Virginia by Jill McCorkle

Novel
F, 20s
Contemporary South
Dramatic

Madge, a perpetually morose woman, casts a light on her character when she reveals to her cousin what happened to her husband eight years ago.

• • •

Hannah, I killed Raymond (...). He held the gun but I pulled the trigger. He begged me. (...)

'If you love me, you'll pull that goddamned (and I quote of course), 'you'll pull that goddamned trigger.' It wasn't love that I was feeling right then. Sometimes I think I was feeling nothing at all. Sometimes I think I was feeling impatient and ready to get it all over with so that I wouldn't have to be ready to put my hands to my ears all the time. He was so weak. It seemed that weakness had covered over or erased every feature on his face. He just wasn't the same man that I fell in love with and met at the end of the River Baptist aisle. I was staring at him there, those eyes like they couldn't focus right, his hand forcing my finger into that hole and up against that cool metal trigger. There was no recollection; I suddenly felt like I might be preparing to kill a bug or a mouse that had frightened me. I was frightened. My hands shook like jelly. 'Do it, do it,' he kept saying over and over. 'Don't be scared to do it.' I did it and it seems to me when I look back that I didn't even hear a noise. (...)

I love you like a sister, Hannah, and I hope you can go right on loving me after knowing all this.

Their Eyes Were Watching God by Zora Neale Hurston

Novel
F, 60+
Central Florida, 1930s
Dramatic

Nanny, a former slave, scolds her grandaughter Janie, who has just come of age. Nanny wants Janie to marry wisely.

• • •

So you don't want to marry off decent like, do you? You just wants to hug and kiss and feel around with first one man and then another, huh? You wants to make me suck de same sorrow yo' mama did, eh? Mah ole head ain't gray enough. Mah back ain't bowed enough to suit yuh! (...)

Come to you' Grandma, honey. Set in her lap lak you' use tuh. Yo' Nanny wouldn't harm a hair uh yo' head. She don't want nobody else to do it neither if she kin help it. Honey, de white man is de ruler of everythin as fur as Ah been able tuh find out. Maybe it's some place way off in de ocean where de black man is in power, but we don't know nothin' but what we see. So de white man throw down de load and tell de nigger man tuh pick it up. He pick it up because he have to, but he don't tote it. He hand it to his womenfolks. De nigger woman is de mule uh de world so fur as Ah can see. Ah been prayin' fuh it tuh be different wid you. Lawd, Lawd, Lawd!

"Toward a Topography of the Parallel Universe" from *Girl, Interrupted* by Susanna Kaysen

Memoir
F, 20+
Contemporary
Dramatic

A former mental patient tells all.

• • •

People ask, How did you get in there? What they really want to know is if they are likely to end up in there as well. I can't answer the real question. All I can tell them is, It's easy.

And it is easy to slip into a parallel universe. There are so many of them: worlds of the insane, the criminal, the crippled, the dying, perhaps of the dead as well. These worlds exist alongside this world and resemble it, but are not in it.

My roommate Georgina came in swiftly and totally, during her junior year at Vassar. She was in a theatre watching a movie when a tidal wave of blackness broke over her head. The entire world was obliterated—for a few minutes. She knew she had gone crazy. (...)

But most people pass over incrementally, making a series of perforations in the membrane between here and there until an opening exists. And who can resist an opening?

In the parallel universe the laws of physics are suspended. What goes up does not necessarily come down, a body at rest does not tend to stay at rest; (...) The very arrangement of molecules is fluid: tables can be clocks, faces, flowers.

These are facts you find out later, though.

Another odd feature of the parallel universe is that although it is invisible from this side, once you are in it you can easily see the world you came from (...).

Every window on Alcatraz has a view of San Francisco.

Ugly Ways by Tina McElroy Ansa

Novel
F, 20s
Contemporary
Dramatic

*To her sisters, Annie Ruth unleashes her true feelings about
their recently dead mother, a powerful, controlling woman
they called "Mudear."*

• • •

Oh, grow the fuck up, Emily (...). If she hated me, she hated you.
She hated you, she hated me, she hated Betty, she hated Poppa,
she hated the house she lived in, she hated Mulberry. She hated all
of us. Don't you really know that? (...)

Sister girls, I don't know about you, but I am sick and tired of a lot
of stuff. I'm so tired of trying to pretend that she was something
she wasn't. I'm so sick of coming home for holidays and sitting
around the dinner table like nothing's wrong. (...)

I'm so sick of pretending that we had something we didn't that I
could just about die myself. But that's just the thing now, 'cause I'm
gonna be a mama now and I want to turn loose some of this crazy
shit. *She's behind us now?* God girl, ya'll expect me to go and have
an abortion, get rid of my child because of the kind of mother we
had. Does that sound like all this, all of Mudear's shit, is *behind us?*
No! I don't want to *not* be a mother because she ruined us. I'm
tired of her ruining my life. I won't have it anymore. And I won't
have her ruining it from the grave.

The Use and Need of the Life of Carry A. Nation by Carry A. Nation

Memoir
F, 50+
1905
Dramatic

Carry A. Nation, the radical Temperance crusader, made a name for herself by physically attacking saloons with bottles, rocks, and hatchets. In her autobiography, she describes her calling to destroy three saloons in Kiowa, Kansas.

• • •

One day I was so sad; I opened the Bible with a prayer for light, and saw these words: "Arise, shine, for thy light is come and the glory of the Lord is risen upon thee." These words gave me unbounded delight. (...)

On the 6th of June, before retiring, as I often did, I threw myself face downward at the foot of my bed and told the Lord to use me any way to suppress the dreadful curse of liquor; that He had ways to do it, that I had done all I knew, that the wicked had conspired to take from us the protection of homes in Kansas; to kill our children and break our hearts ...The next morning, before I awoke, I heard these words very distinctly: "Go to Kiowa, and (as in a vision, my hands were lifted and cast down suddenly) I'll stand by you." I did not hear these words as other words; there was no voice, but they seemed to be spoken in my heart. I sprang from my bed as if electrified, and knew this was direction given me, for I understood that it was God's will for me to go to Kiowa to break, or smash, the saloons.

A Vain Treasure by Becky Kohn

Novel
F, 15
Cairo, 1014
Dramatic

Dalal, the daughter of a wealthy Jewish doctor living in Muslim Cairo, recollects the night her brother's wife went into labor. Dalal fears that the child will die—as did the first—because several years earlier, in a fit of jealousy, she had cursed their future children.

• • •

Grievous was the news. For though it was at least a month before her time, Hayfa had gone into labor. Nor could I but anticipate the worst outcome and blame myself.

Never would my brother's wife give birth to a healthy child! Not while I yet lived amongst them.

Yet where could I go?

I fled to my room. And while the others gathered what medical items they might need, and a slave left to rouse the midwife, and my nurse stood in the passageway outside our sleeping rooms invoking God's mercy with whatever prayers came to her lips, I wept. Indeed, had my spirit been in my hand I doubt not that I would have given it up.

Later, I awoke as one startled by a noise, though I hear nothing. How long have I been asleep? I know not. Indeed, I recollect not so much as having put my cheek to the pillow. Yet, from the faintest light visible through the window-screen, I gather the time to be between dawn and sunrise, the first Muslim prayer period. Indeed, perhaps I have been awoken by the call of a muezzin from one of the little mosques nearby.

My head aches and my eyes are swollen; mementos of the previous night's weeping. I stumble the short distance from my matarba to the basin, where I pour some water from the pitcher and, without uttering even a single prayer—may God forgive me—wash my hands and bathe my stinging eyes. And then do I creep to the doorway, part the drapery, and listen.

Naught but my own breathing do I hear, a stillness unusual for the household at daybreak. For since my earliest memory has it been the custom in Father's household to begin the day at first light. And here, in the doorway, I hesitate, afraid to seek out that which surely I wish not to know.

"Velocity vs. Viscosity" from *Girl, Interrupted* by Susanna Kaysen

Memoir
F, 20+
Contemporary
Dramatic

A former mental patient offers her expert opinion.

• • •

Insanity comes in two basic varieties: slow and fast.

I'm not talking about onset or duration. I mean the quality of the insanity, the day-to-day business of being nuts.

There are a lot of names: depression, catatonia, mania, anxiety, agitation. They don't tell you much.

The predominant quality of the slow form is viscosity.

Experience is thick. Perceptions are thickened and dulled. Time is slow, dripping slowly through the clogged filter of thickened perception. The body temperature is low. The pulse is sluggish. The immune system is half-asleep. The organism is torpid and brackish. Even the reflexes are diminished, as if the lower leg couldn't be bothered to jerk itself out of its stupor when the knee is tapped.

Viscosity occurs on a cellular level. And so does velocity.

In contrast to viscosity's cellular coma, velocity endows every platelet and muscle fiber with a mind of its own, a means of knowing and commenting on its own behavior. There is too much perception, and beyond the plethora of perceptions, a plethora of thoughts about the perceptions and about the fact of having perceptions. Digestion could kill you! What I mean is the unceasing awareness of the processes of digestion could exhaust you to death. And digestion is just an involuntary sideline to thinking, which is where the real trouble begins.

Waiting by Ha Jin

Novel
F, 50+
Contemporary China
Seriocomic

Shuyu, an old-fashioned woman, defends her bound, concealed feet to modern Chinese women.

• • •

You know girls, only my man's allowed to see them. (...) That's the rule. (...) You know, take off your shoes and socks is like open your pants. (...) 'Cause you bound your feet only for your future husband, not for other men, to make your feet more precious to your man. By the way, do you know what this was called in the old days? (...) It's called Golden Lotus, like a treasure. (...)

Of course it hurt. Don't tell me about pain. I started to bind my feet when I was seven. My heavens, for two years I'd weep in pain every night. In the summer my toes swelled up, filled with pus, and the flesh rotted, but I dared not loosen the binding. My mother'd whack me with a big bamboo slat if she found me doing that. Whenever I ate fish, the pus in my heels dripped out. There's the saying goes, 'Every pair of lotus feet come from a bucket of tears.' (...)

Mother said it's my second chance to marry good, 'cause my face ugly. You know, men are crazy about lotus feet in those days. The smaller your feet are, the better looking you are to them.

Waiting to Exhale by Terry McMillan

Novel
F, 30s
Phoenix, Arizona. Contemporary
Dramatic

Gloria, a single African-American mother, tells her sixteen-year-old son the facts of life.

• • •

Tarik (...). Let me ask you something. And don't lie to me. Are you using condoms? (...)

Most of the time? (...)

I want you to listen to me, and you listen to me good. You do not—you understand me—you do not walk out of this house from this day forward without your house key and a condom in your wallet. (...) And you do not, under any circumstances, believe a damn word any of these sweet little innocent girls tell you when they say they're using something. (...)

Tarik (...) listen to me (...). This phone rings off the hook with nothin' but girls on the other end, and I'm not saying anything is wrong with that. I'm not saying having sex at your age is wrong, either. But some of these teenage girls are dizzy as hell, their mamas don't teach them anything, and some of them don't think any further than today, let alone tomorrow (...). For some of these girls, the only thing in their future is a baby. And Lord knows you could make some pretty ones. I just don't want you to be so naive and take their word for it when they tell you they're on the pill or any nonsense like that. You protect yourself, you hear me?

Waiting to Exhale by Terry McMillan

Novel
F, 37
Phoenix, Arizona. Contemporary
Seriocomic

*Tired of her on-again, off-again relationship with Kenneth,
a perpetually "about to be divorced" man, Savannah finally
ends it.*

• • •

Can I ask you something? (...) Have you filed for your divorce?

[Not yet.]

I figured as much. But you want me to meet you in Palm Springs so
you can fuck my brains out for three days and then go home to
your wife, and a month or two later, you'll call me up all pitiful and
probably say something like, even though you *love* me to death,
you can't leave your wife right now because you'd feel too guilty
about leaving your kid, or it's too much money involved, or whatever
other excuses you motherfuckers always manage to come up with.
(...)

Look Kenneth. I'm thirty-seven years old. I've got enough shit going
on in my life right now to deal with, without putting my life on hold
waiting for you to divorce your wife, okay? Why do you guys always
pull this shit? You claim you're miserable, so you fuck around on
your wife and then expect the other woman to wait for you to final-
ize your goddamn plans. You must be nuts. Now, I'm sure there's
plenty of women out here who'd probably jump at this chance.
Because I guess you fit in that category of what's commonly known
as a 'good catch.' But I'm not one of them. I'm not that desperate.
(...)

Would you give me a courtesy, since we're talking courtesy here?
(...)

Leave me the fuck alone.

"A Walled Garden" from *The Old Forest and Other Stories* by Peter Taylor

Short story
F, 50+
American South, Contemporary
Seriocomic

A genteel Southern woman speaks to her daughter's suitor from her walled garden.

• • •

You understand, my daughter has finally made her life with me in this little garden plot, and year by year she has come to realize how little else there is hereabouts to compare with it.

And you, you know nothing of flowers? A young man who doesn't know the zinnia from the aster! How curious that you and my daughter should have made friends. I don't know under what circumstances you two may have met. In her League work, no doubt. She throws herself so into whatever work she undertakes. Oh? Why, of course, I should have guessed. She simply spent herself on the Chest Drive this year .... But my daughter has most of her permanent friends among the flower-minded people. She makes so few friends nowadays outside of our little circle, sees so few people outside our own garden here, really, that I find it quite strange for there to be someone who doesn't know flowers.

No, nothing, we've come to feel, is ever very lovely, really lovely, I mean, in this part of the nation, nothing but this garden …

"The Waltz" from *The Portable Dorothy Parker* by Dorothy Parker

Short story
F, 25+
A dance floor, 1930s
Comic

A woman laments having been asked to dance.

• • •

And I had to go and tell him that I'd adore to dance with him. I cannot understand why I wasn't struck right down dead. Yes, and being struck dead would look like a day in the country, compared to struggling out a dance with this boy. But what could I do? Everyone else at the table had got up to dance, except him and me. There was I, trapped. Trapped like a trap in a trap.

What can you say, when a man asks you to dance with him? I most certainly will not dance with you, I'll see you in hell first. Why, thank you, I'd like to awfully, but I'm having labor pains. Oh yes, do let's dance together—it's so nice to meet a man who isn't a scaredy-cat about catching my beri-beri. No. There was nothing for me to do, but say I'd adore to. Well, we might as well get it over with. All right, Cannonball, let's run out on the field. You won the toss; you can lead.

"What Happened" by Kathryn Eberly

Short story
F, 20s
Contemporary
Seriocomic

A woman tells the story of her friend, Esperanza.

• • •

[What Happened] Was that my friend Esperanza got pulled over for speeding and she was driving her little blue Honda with the dent in the left fender seventy miles per hour on a steep hill and over the bump and she got caught. I was scared shitless as she kept on yelling, prick, prick, prick in that accent of hers, prick, as the cop approached and she rolled down her window saying hello officer and not very polite either. Well, she got a fifty dollar ticket and the cop ran a check on her and he found eight hundred dollars worth of unpaid fines so he impounded the car and we took the number 24 bus home. She was pissed off but it all ended up OK meaning she got the car back. Of course she had to appear in court and came out of it with 200 hours of community service and a stern talking to. She kept right on parking in those red zones. Also, Esperanza had a handicapped parking sticker and she used that sometimes. I was so embarrassed but I went along with it. She could make me laugh so hard I'd practically bust a gut but she scared me too with her outbursts or when we did those U-turns or a sudden screech to a stop. Much later when I found out I couldn't possibly imagine it, her death, I mean. No, it wasn't a car crash, she took the pills and it wasn't any accident. Everyone was so shocked because Esie was so funny all the time but she was illegal too. You know, no one ever mentioned how terrified she must have been about getting deported especially her being a dyke and all.

"What the Living Do" by Marie Howe

Poem
F, 20+
Contemporary, Cambridge, Massachusetts
Dramatic

*The speaker celebrates life by addressing Johnny, a friend
presumed dead.*

• • •

Johnny, the kitchen sink has been clogged for days, some utensil
probably fell down there. And the Drano won't work but smells
dangerous, and the crusty dishes have piled up

waiting for the plumber I still haven't called. This is the everyday we
spoke of. It's winter again: the sky's a deep, headstrong blue, and
the sunlight pours

through the open living-room windows because the heat's on too
high in here and I can't turn it off. For weeks now, driving, or drop-
ping a bag of groceries in the street, the bag breaking,

I've been thinking: This is what the living do. And yesterday, hurry-
ing along those wobbly bricks in the Cambridge sidewalk, spilling
my coffee down my wrist and sleeve,

I thought it again, and again later, when buying a hairbrush: This is
it. Parking. Slamming the car door shut in the cold. What you called
that yearning.

What you finally gave up. We want the spring to come and the winter to pass. We want whoever to call or not call, a letter a kiss—we
want more and more and
then more of it.

But there are moments, walking, when I catch a glimpse of myself
in the window glass, say, the window of the corner video store, and

I'm gripped by a cherishing so deep

for my own blowing hair, chapped face, and unbuttoned coat that
I'm speechless: I am living. I remember you.

White Bird in a Blizzard
by Laura Kasischke

Novel
F, 20+
Garden Heights, Ohio, 1985
Dramatic

Katrina's mother, Eve, has vanished.

• • •

I am sixteen when my mother steps out of her skin one frozen
January afternoon—pure self, atoms twinkling like microscopic dia-
mond chips around her, perhaps the chiming of a clock, or a few
bright flute notes in the distance—and disappears.

No one sees her leave, but she is gone.

Only the morning before, my mother was a housewife—a housewife who, for twenty years, kept our house as swept up and sterile
as the mind of winter itself, so perhaps she finally just whisk-
broomed herself out, a luminous cloud of her drifing through the
bedroom window as soft as talcum powder, mingling with the
snowflakes as they fell, and the stardust and the lunar ash out
there.

Her name is Eve, and this is Garden Heights, Ohio, so I used to like
to think of my mother as Eve—the naked one, the first one—when
she was in the Garden, poisoning the weeds with bleach, defoliat-
ing the trees, stuffing their leaves down the garbage disposal, then
scouring the sink with something chemical and harsh, but pow-
dered, something dyed ocean blue to disguise its deadly powers for
the housewives like my mother who bought it, only dimly realizing
that what they'd purchased with its snappy name (Spic and Span,
Mr, Clean, Fantastik) was pure acid.

The blue of a child's eyes, the blue of a robin's egg—But swallow a teaspoon of that and it will turn your intestines to lace.

This Eve, like the first one, was bored in Garden Heights. She spent her afternoons in the silence of a house she'd just cleaned yesterday from bottom to top, and there was nothing left for her to do beyond planning the nothing of the future, too.

White Bird in a Blizzard
by Laura Kasischke

Novel
F, 17
Garden Heights, Ohio, 1983
Dramatic

Katrina draws comparisons between her psychiatrist and her mother.

• • •

"How are things with Phil?" Dr. Phaler asks ten minutes before my hour's up. By now, we have entirely dispensed with the pretense of psychoanalysis (...).

It is like gossiping once a week with a friend, except that the gossip is about me.

And, for a hundred dollars an hour, Dr. Phaler is a good dispenser of lightweight advice. She never seems distracted. She monitors her facial expressions for just the right display of detachment and compassion, and she always remembers the names of the minor characters in my life—my chemistry teacher, my friends Beth and Mickey (...)

Dr. Phaler is like the mother you always wished you had. The mother you would have been perfectly happy to pay a hundred dollars an hour to have. Except that you could never afford such a mother. If you had to *buy* a mother, you'd end up with some old lady who lived with a dozen other kids in a trailer. Or a mother who'd get sick of you and leave, like the one I had.

Whores for Gloria
by William T. Vollmann

Novel
F, 20+
Contemporary
Dramatic

Peggy, a whore, recalls a trick.

• • •

One time, (...) I picked up this *real* nice, clean-cut man, but he was *built*, really built good. I got him up into my motel room and he told me he as a hit man. He *murdered* people for a living. All he wanted to do was talk. When he told me his profession I thought, *mmmarvelous*! The things I got myself into, right? All he wanted to do was talk about the people he killed, how sorry he was that he had to do it, but it was his job. He told me a few little details, an' I was really on pins and needles. (...)

Now the man's armed, so I was pretty shook up. But I acted real calm and I kept the conversation goin' and that's just about all you really need to do to keep your safety. Never let them know that you're gonna panic or you don't want their company—and he had *paid* me for that half-hour that he wanted to talk. That really tripped me out when somebody knocked on the door. He jumped up off the bed drew his gun. I didn't know if he was gonna put *rounds* in it or what. I said sit down an' *relax*, whoever's at my door I'm not gonna open it, just gonna tell them through the door that I'm busy and to get on. So I did that, but I mean that was a real spooky experience.

Whores for Gloria
by William T. Vollmann

Novel
F, 20+
Contemporary
Dramatic

Dinah, an African-American whore, talks about the life.

• • •

OK, now, there been times when girls have gotten killed; the Vice have come by with pictures and stuff and showed 'em to us, like the Green River Killer when we were up in Seattle. There been times when I've cut (...). I've had to cut guys. Lot of 'em were, that's when I were drinkin; that when I would get upset. Get vi'lent. 'Cause they'd get vi'lent with me. There was actually a time when I begged, actually begged this one guy not to get vi'lent with me, 'cause I knew what I would do. It's happened plenty of times, believe me. This one guy, when I begged him, actually begged him not to get vi'lent with me, and I pleaded and I started crying because I was in such a depressed state of mind that I didn't care. So he wanted to get vi'lent with me, so I just started stabbing him. He went to the hospital; we both went in an ambulance, 'cause he pushed me through a two-storey window. I didn't go out the bottom floor; I just went out the large window, and I took off running and he came running up and he fell, and I waited for the police, and they found me, and they held me in jail twenty-one days to see if he died. Then they let me go, 'cause there were no charges or anything. It was self-defense.

"The Wife of Bath" from *The Canterbury Tales* by Geoffrey Chaucer, translated by Nevill Coghill

Epic poem
F, 30s
English countryside, circa 1386
Comic

A group of travelers, on horseback, pass the time riding to Canterbury and back by telling tales, in turn. The Wife of Bath is a member of this entourage.

• • •

If there were no authority on earth
Except experience, mine, for what it's worth,
And that's enough for me, all goes to show
That marriage is a misery and a woe;
For let me say, if I may make so bold,
My lords, since when I was but twelve years old,
Thanks be to God Eternal evermore,
Five husbands have I had at the church door;
yes, it's a fact that I have had so many,
All worthy in their way, as good as any.
      Someone said recently for my persuasion
That as Christ only went on one occasion
To grace a wedding in Cana of Galilee
He taught me by example there to see
That it is wrong to marry more than once.
Consider, too, how sharply, for the nonce,
He spoke, rebuking the Samaritan
Beside the well, Christ Jesus, God and man.
      "Thou has had five husbands unto thee
And he that even now thou hast," said He,
"is not thy husband." Such the words that fell;
But what he meant thereby I cannot tell.
No lawful spouse to the Samaritan?

How many might have had her, then, to wife?
I've never heard an answer all my life
To give the number final definition.
People may guess or frame a supposition,
But I can say for certain, it's no lie,
God bade us all to wax and multiply.
That kindly text I well can understand.
Is not my husband under God's command
To leave his father and mother and take me?
No word of what the number was to be,
Then why not marry two or even eight?
And why speak evil of the married state?
          Take wise King Solomon of long ago;
We hear he had a thousand wives or so.
And would to God it were allowed to me
To be refreshed, aye, half so much as he!

"A Wilderness Station" from *Open Secrets* by Alice Munro

Short story
F, 20s
Walley Goal, Ontario, Canada, 1853
Dramatic

Annie McKillop is the mail-order bride of Simon, the dead man described here; George is Simon's younger brother.

• • •

George came dragging him across the snow I thought it was a log he dragged. I didn't know it was him. George said, it's him. A branch fell out of a tree and hit him, he said. He didn't say he was dead. I looked for him to speak. His mouth was part way open with snow in it. Also his eyes part way open. We had to get inside because it was starting to storm like anything. (...) Inside where I had the fire going it was warm and the snow started melting off him. His blood thawed and ran a little around his ear. I didn't know what to do and I was afraid to go near him. I thought his eyes were watching me.

George sat by the fire with his big heavy coat on and his boots on. He was turned away. (...) I said, how do you know if he is dead? George said, touch him if you want to know. But I would not. Outside there was terrible storming, the wind in the trees and over top of our roof. I said, Our Father who art in Heaven, and that was how I got my courage. (...) George never turned around or paid attention or helped me when I asked. I didn't take the trousers or coat off of him, I couldn't manage.(...) So I went and pulled George by his arm. Help me, I said. What? he said. I said we had to turn him. So he came and helped me and we got him turned over, he was laying face down. And then I saw, I saw where the axe had cut.

"A Wilderness Station" from *Open Secrets* by Alice Munro

Short story
F, 20s
Walley Goal, Ontario, Canada, 1853
Dramatic

Here, Annie appeals to George, who has just killed his brother, Simon.

• • •

Listen, George. Listen to me.

If you own up what do you think will happen? They will hang you. You will be dead, you will be no good to anybody. What will become of your land? Likely it will all go back to the Crown and somebody else will get it and all the work you have done will be for them.

What will become of me here if you are took away? (...)

Listen, I know things. I am older than you are. I am religious too, I pray to God every night and my prayers are answered. I know what God wants as well as any preacher knows and I know that he does not want a good lad like you to be hanged. All you have to do is say you are sorry. Say you are sorry and mean it well and God will forgive you. I will say the same thing, I am sorry too because when I saw he was dead I did not wish, not one minute, for him to be alive. I will say, God forgive me, and you do the same. Kneel down. (...)

All right. I have an idea. I am going to get the Bible. (...) do you believe in the Bible? Say you do. Nod your head. (...)

There. There you did. Now. I am going to do what we all used to do in the Home when we wanted to know what would happen to us or what we should do in our life. We would open the Bible any place and poke our finger at a page and then open our eyes and read the verse (...). To make double sure of it just say when you close your eyes, God guide my finger. (...)

All right, I'll do it for you.

Women Love Sex by Linda Jaivin

Essay
F, 25+
Contemporary
Comic

A woman defends her love of sex.

• • •

I'd like to set the record straight. I am one of those women who love sex. This is something that women are still not supposed to admit in polite society.(…)

Ever since Eve copped the rap for getting her and Addie thrown out of Paradise, women have been forced to protest 'I'm not Eve! I'm not Eve! I'm a good girl.' The ladies doth protest too much, methinks. Give me Mae West any day. She's no lady, and I much prefer her attitude: 'A hard man is good to find.' 'I was Snow White...but I drifted.' (….)

I'm not putting down romantic love. I love love as much as the next girl, especially when I'm getting heaps. But the fact of the matter is, some women love sex more than they love love, some love love more than they love sex, some love them both at once, some keep 'em separated, some love one on Monday and the other on Tuesday, and then there are women who would rather stay at home any day and read a book instead—

"The Yellow Wall-paper" by Charlotte Perkins Gilman

Short story
F, 25+
New England, 1892
Dramatic

A young wife is held hostage, under pretext of rest and relaxation, by her husband.

• • •

John laughs at me, of course, but one expects that in marriage.

John is a physician, and *perhaps*—(I would not say it to a living soul, of course, but this is dead paper and a great relief to my mind—) *perhaps* that is one reason I do not get well faster.

You see he does not believe I am sick!

And what can one do?

If a physician of high standing, and one's own husband, assures friends and relatives that there is really nothing the matter with one but temporary nervous depression—a slight hysterical tendency— what is one to do?

My brother is also a physician, and also of high standing, and he says the same thing.

So I take phosphates or phosphites—whichever it is, and tonics, (...) and I am absolutely forbidden to "work" until I am well again.

Personally, I disagree with their ideas.

Personally, I believe that congenial work, with excitement and change, would do me good.

But what is one to do?

I did write for a while in spite of them; but it *does* exhaust me a good deal—having to be so sly about it, or else meet with heavy opposition.(...)

I sometimes fancy that in my condition if I had less opposition and more society and stimulus—but John says the very worst thing I can do is to think about my condition, and I confess it always makes me feel bad.(...)

There comes John, and I must put this away,—he hates to have me write a word.

"You Were Perfectly Fine" by Dorothy Parker

Short story
F, 25+
1930s
Comic

A woman assures last night's date that he did not drink too much nor behave foolishly. She knows, of course, that he was perfectly horrible.

• • •

Good heavens, no. Everyone thought you terribly funny. Of course, Jim Pierson was a little stuffy, there for a minute at dinner. But people sort of held him back in his chair, and got him calmed down. I don't think anybody at the other tables noticed it at all. Hardly anybody. (...)

You were perfectly fine. But you know how silly Jim gets, when he thinks anybody is making too much fuss over Elinor. (...) You were only fooling, that's all. She thought you were awfully amusing. She was having a marvelous time. She only got a little tiny bit annoyed just once, when you poured the clam-juice down her back. (...) Oh, she'll be alright. Just send her some flowers or something. Don't worry about it. It isn't anything. (...)

You were fine(...) Everybody was crazy about you. The maitre d'hotel was a little worried because you wouldn't stop singing, but he really didn't mind. All he said was, he was afraid they'd close the place again, if there was so much noise. But he didn't care a bit, himself. I think he loved seeing you have such a good time. Oh, you were just singing away, there, for about an hour. It wasn't so terribly loud, at all. (...) You were wonderful. We were all trying to make you stop singing for a minute, and eat something, but you wouldn't hear of it. My, you were funny.

Men's
Monologues

"Adirondack Iron" from *Rule of the Bone* by Russell Banks

Novel
M, 14
AuSable, upstate New York, 1994
Seriocomic

Bone shares his attitude toward "persons of authority"

• • •

(...) don't bother your parents and don't bother the cops or one of them will sic the other on you. All I had to do was stay out of the way of both and not flag either by going back to school who didn't want me anyhow (...) even the cops know that a little weed can't hurt anybody. Most of them when they bust you are only trying to score for themselves anyhow and once they take your stash if you lick their boots and promise never to smoke reefer again so long as you live and thank them for saving you from a life of drug addiction and criminality they keep your drugs and let you go. Unless they're after you for something else you're not worth the paperwork. I've learned that's generally true of life, if you're not worth the paperwork adults won't hassle you. Except for the truly dumb and the nutcases of course, people who act on principle. They'll hassle you.

Affliction by Russell Banks

Novel
M, 40s
New Hampshire. Contemporary
Dramatic

Wade, a divorced man, is trying to console his young daughter after picking her up too late to take her trick-or-treating.

• • •

I'm sorry for the screwup (...). But I couldn't help it that it's too late to go trick-or-treating now. I couldn't help it I had to stop at Penney's for the costume (...). And you were hungry, remember.

Can't you see...look out there...Can't you see that nobody's got their porch lights on anymore? It's late; it's too late now. Those Hoyt kids, they're just out to get in trouble. See (...). They put shaving cream all over that mailbox there. And they chopped down all of Herb Crane's new bushes. Damn (...). Those damned kids tipped over Harrison's toolshed. Jesus Christ. (...)

Look, they cut the Annises' clotheslines, and I bet there's hell of a lot more they done out back where you can't see it (...). And there, see all those smashed flowerpots? Little bastards. Jesus H. Christ. (...)

See, honey, that's all that's going on out there now. (...) You don't want to deal with that kind of stuff, do you? Trick-or-treating's over, I'm sorry to say.

Affliction by Russell Banks

Novel
M, 40s
New Hampshire. Contemporary
Dramatic

*Suffering from an abscessed tooth, a troublesome time with
his small daughter, and an interfering ex-wife, Wade complains to his girlfriend, Margie.*

• • •

Lillian's been trying to nail me to a cross since the day I met her.
Since fucking high school. No. I'm gonna hire me a fucking lawyer
from Concord and get this thing, this divorce thing, rearranged. I
am. I been thinking about it, a lot. I was too fucked up and all,
when we got the divorce, so I just hid out and took whatever
crumbs they were willing to toss me, her and that goddamned
lawyer of hers (...). I didn't even have a regular divorce lawyer, that's
how dumb and fucked up I was. I'm embarrassed to say it, but it's
true. And now she can do any goddamned thing she wants, anything—move to Concord, get married. Move to fucking California, if
she wants. Meanwhile, I still got to send her three hundred bucks a
month child support or go directly to jail, do not pass go. Only,
when it come to actually being with my own kid, being a real father
and all, I don't have a single say-so (...) It's like she owns Jill or
something and only loans her out to me or something, and then
only when she feels like it. And when she wants her back, she
comes and gets her. Like last night. That's not right (...). People
aren't property. Nobody owns anybody, especially not kids. Right's
right.

The Age of Grief by Jane Smiley

Novella
M, 35
Contemporary
Dramatic

Dave, a dentist, takes measure of his life.

• • •

I am thirty-five years old, and it seems to me that I have arrived at the age of grief. Others arrive there sooner. Almost no one arrives much later. (...)

It is not only that we know that love ends, children are stolen, parents die feeling that their lives have been meaningless. It is not only that, by this time, a lot of acquaintances and friends have died and all the others are getting ready to sooner or later. It is more that the barriers between the circumstances of oneself and the rest of the world have broken down (...). I understand that later you come to an age of hope, or at least resignation. I suspect it takes a long time to get there. (...)

So how does the certainty that your wife loves another man feel? (...) I have to admit I don't remember much Gray's *Anatomy,* so I don't know why it feels the way it feels, as if all your flesh were squeezing together, squeezing the air out of your lungs, squeezing the alveoli so they can never inflate again. More than that, it is as if soon there might be no spaces left inside at all, no conduits for fluids, even. Only the weight of solid flesh, the conscious act of picking up this heavy foot, and then this heavy foot, reaching this cumbersome hand so slowly that the will to grasp is lost before the object is touched.

The Age of Grief by Jane Smiley

Novella
M, 30+
Contemporary
Seriocomic

A "pugnacious" patient visits the dentist.

• • •

I don't know (...). Things are more fucked every day. (...)

I mean, I don't know why I'm sitting here having my teeth fixed. It's going to cost me a lot of money that I could spend having the other stuff fixed. By the way, don't touch the front teeth. I play the trumpet, and if you touch the front teeth, then I'll have to change my embouchure. (...)

Well, I'm not sure I *want* to open. I mean, if you don't do anything, then I can spend my money on therapy or something that might really improve my life. (...)

My wife made this appointment for me. Now I've lost my job, and she's kicked me out. But she sent me this little card, telling me to go here, and I came. I mean, I can't— (...) I can't believe she kicked me out, but I really can't believe she cares whether or not I got to the dentist. (...)

Just let me talk. I'll pay you. (...) I'll pay you the money I should be paying a psychiatrist. (...)

[pause] Hey, I don't know. Go ahead and fill a couple of teeth. You're probably better at that, anyway.

"Ali, the Wonder Boy" from *The Muhammad Ali Reader* by Gerald Early

Essay
M, 40s
Contemporary
Dramatic

A man remembers the summer he was fourteen years old, the last year he played baseball regularly. Muhammad Ali was his hero then.

• • •

I was no good at woodworking and the like, so I saved my paper route money and simply bought a bat, the best bat I could find, a genuine Louisville Slugger, the first one I ever owned. I sanded that bat, restained it dark, retaped the handle, and decided to give it a name. I carefully carved, scratched, really, into the bat the word "Ali." (...). I called the bat "the Great Ali."

I used that bat for the entire summer and a magical season it was. I was the best hitter in the neighborhood. I had a career year. There was no pitch I couldn't hit. At the plate, I could do no wrong. Doubles, triples, home runs. I could hit at will. (...)

In any case, the bat broke. Some kid used it without my permission. He hit a foul ball and the bat split, the barrel flying one way, the splintered handle still in the kid's hands. It was the end of the Great Ali.

"Amores: Book I from Amores" by Ovid, translated by Guy Lee

Poem
M, 20+
Ancient Rome
Comic

A lover teaches his lady silent signals for use when they are at a dinner with her husband. (Romans, like the Greeks, did not sit down to dinner; they reclined on couches.)

• • •

Your husband? Going to the same dinner as us?
I hope it chokes him.

So I'm only to gaze at you, darling? Play gooseberry
While another man enjoys your touch?

You'll lie there snuggling up to him? He'll put his arm
round your neck whenever he wants? (...)

However here's my plan. Listen carefully.
Don't throw my words of wisdom to the winds.

Arrive before him—not that I see what good
arriving first will do but arrive first all the same.

When he takes his place on the couch and you go to join him
looking angelic, secretly touch my foot.

Watch me for nods and looks that talk
and unobserved return my signals

in the language of eyebrows and fingers
with annotations in wine.
Whenever you think of our love-making

stroke that rosy cheek with your thumb.
If you're cross with me, darling,
press the lobe of your ear

but turn your ring round if you're pleased
with anything I say or do.

When you feel like cursing your fool of a husband
touch the table as if you were praying.

(...)

Refuse all food he has tasted first—
It has touched his lips.

Don't lean your gentle head against his shoulder
and don't let him embrace you

or slide a hand inside your dress
or touch your breasts. Above all don't kiss him.
(...)

But whatever happens tonight tell me tomorrow
you didn't sleep with him—and stick to that story.

The Apology by Plato from *Classical Rhetoric and its Christian and Secular Tradition from Ancient to Modern Times* by George A. Kennedy

Essay
M, 70
Ancient Greece
Dramatic

Having been sentenced to die (for corrupting youth and atheism), Socrates addresses his accusers.

• • •

Perhaps, gentlemen of the jury, you think that I have been convicted because of a lack of the kind of words by which I would have persuaded you if I had thought it right to do and say everything so as to escape the charge. Far from it. I have been convicted by a lack of daring and shamelessness and of wanting to say to you the kinds of things which you most like to hear: you would have liked me to wail and carry on and do and say lots of things unworthy of me in my own judgment. This is what others have accustomed you to hear. But during the trial I didn't think I should do anything slavish and I have no regrets now at the nature of my defense; indeed, I much prefer to die after a defense like this than to live after another kind of defense. Neither in court nor in battle should I, nor anyone else, fight in order to avoid death at any cost (…) Avoiding death, gentlemen, is probably not very difficult; it is much more difficult to avoid doing wrong (…). Now having been condemned to death I leave you, but my opponents leave having been convicted by the Truth of wickedness and injustice. I stick with my punishment and they can have theirs.

"Araby" by James Joyce

Short story
M, young adult, recalling prepubescence
Ireland, 1910
Dramatic

*A young man recalls watching Mangan's sister, his first love,
and the explosive feelings her visage stirred in him.*

• • •

Every morning I lay on the floor in the front parlour watching her
door. The blind was pulled down to within an inch of the sash so
that I could not be seen. When she came out on the doorstep my
heart leaped. I ran to the hall, seized my books and followed her. I
kept her brown figure always in my eye and, when we came near
the point at which our ways diverged, I quickened my pace and
passed her. This happened morning after morning. I had never spoken to her, except for a few casual words, and yet her name was
like a summons to all my foolish blood.

Her image accompanied me even in places the most hostile to
romance. On Saturday evenings when my aunt went marketing I
had to go to carry some of the parcels. We walked through the flaring streets, jostled by drunken men and bargaining women, amid
the curses of labourers, the shrill litanies of shop-boys (...). These
noises converged in a single sensation of life for me: I imagined that
I bore my chalice safely through a throng of foes. Her name sprang
to my lips at moments in strange prayers and praises which I myself
did not understand. My eyes were often full of tears (I could not
tell why) and at times a flood from my heart seemed to pour itself
out into my bosom. I thought little of the future. I did not know
whether I would ever speak to her or not or, if I spoke to her, how I
could tell her of my confused adoration. But my body was like a
harp and her words and gestures were like fingers running upon the
wires.

"The Artist" from *Acid* by Ed Falco

Short story
M, 40s
Long Island, Contemporary
Dramatic

Tony visits an old pal from his drug days to enlist his help in dealing with a crazed mutual friend, who wants Tony dead. Tony talks as they drive toward their destination.

• • •

I've got a problem. (...)

Just listen a minute (...). I need you to do me this favor, but you have to understand about Ellis. You can't tell just to look at him (...). We're almost there (...). I'll tell you a few things. (...)

Ellis owns this building; he lives on the top floor—the whole floor. He's got a freezer set up in the living room. He'll show it to you. He shows it to everybody. When he opens it, you're going to see a cop (...). Take this exit. (...)

A dead cop. (...)

Could I make this shit up, Jimmy? Really? Ask yourself, if I were lying, would I tell you shit this wild? (...) I'm getting nervous just coming up here (...). I haven't told you half of it (...). He sleeps with little girls from the neighborhood. He pays their junky mothers with shit and they come over in the morning and bathe him—these three little girls. They carry water to his bath. I'm talking eight, nine years old. Same thing at night. It's like some sort of ceremony, some sort of ritual. They fill the tub and then(...) He wants me dead, Jimmy, and the guys' a stone-cold, pure-fucking-insane murderer. He's got this machete (...). Turn right here. (...)

Shit. He's going to fuck me over, man. I know it.

"Babylon Revisited"
by F. Scott Fitzgerald

Short story
M, 35
Paris, 1931
Dramatic

Charlie speaks to his sister-in-law and her husband about reclaiming custody of his daughter, Honoria, a few years after his wife's death and his subsequent stay in a sanitarium.

• • •

I suppose you know what I want to see you about—why I really came to Paris. (...)

I'm awfully anxious to have a home, and I'm awfully anxious to have Honoria in it. I appreciate your taking in Honoria for her mother's sake, but things have changed now—(he hesitated then continued more forcefully)—changed radically with me, and I want to ask you to reconsider the matter. It would be silly for me to deny that about three years ago I was acting badly— (...)

—but all that's over. As I told you, I haven't had more than a drink a day for over a year, and I take that drink deliberately, so that the idea of alcohol won't get too big in my imagination. You see the idea? (...)

Sometimes I forget and don't take it. But I try to take it. Anyhow, I couldn't afford to drink in my position. The people I represent are more than satisfied with what I've done, and I'm bringing my sister over from Burlington to keep house for me, and I want awfully to have Honoria too. You know that even when her mother and I weren't getting along well we never let anything that happened touch Honoria. I know she's fond of me and I know I'm able to take care of her and—well, there you are.

How do you feel about it?

The Basketball Diaries
by Jim Carroll

Memoir
M, 15
Upper Manhattan, summer, 1964
Seriocomic

A disaffected teen tells a tale about losing his summer job.

• • •

I got canned from my shitty job at Yankee Stadium tonight and I couldn't care less. As usual I got the worst product in the joint to hustle: ice cream. Not that ice cream is the worst in general, popcorn is the general bummer; but tonight was about 20 degrees and drizzly out, and even the fruits in this place ain't that fruity. So I'm going through the usual motions in the upper deck, only good thing happening was this blonde in section 20 throwing this gigantic spread a few rows up, perfect eye-to-beaver position. Black panties and all. Then the rain lets go harder and the ground crew shuffles out and covers the field (...). I head up too and two chicks call me over for a sale. I knew it could not be just the ice cream they wanted so I sit down and rap. Turns out they smoke grass and all, or so they say, and I'm getting on o.k. with them, having a smoke and sitting back without that fucking ice box on my back. Then along comes Mr. Balls-buster himself, Rudy the foreman. This prick sneaks constantly around the ballpark checking up on dudes goofing off and I'm one of his prize targets. (...) This time he got me clean, busting about ten regulations, but sitting on the job is the absolute no-no. Only one hope, I leave the box there and try to make a run for it, hoping he can't make out my face or badge number if I can make it down to the lower deck. It's an extra added attraction for the fans and the whole upper deck is cheering me on to outrun the Kaiser in this ridiculous scene.

The Basketball Diaries
by Jim Carroll

Memoir
M, 16
Fall, 1965
Dramatic

The speaker is a prep school basketball star, addicted to heroin.

• • •

Lately my scene at home has dissolved to total bullshit. What to say? My old man gets home at six every day, eats, takes off his shoes and sits in his chair with his pants rolled up and his varicose veins sticking out with his feet up on the stool and he bitches. He bitches about how my hair's too long, that the protesters suck, about nigger this and spic that, the same old shit and I don't answer 'cause he don't listen anyway. It's all so simple it's the most complicated shit I ever had to put up with. Then I got my old lady always trying to bait me into political debates as soon as the news pops on and if I bite and argue then the whole house is a screaming maniac nuthouse and if I don't bother it's even worse. And I don't bother anymore. I just refuse to give the slightest fuck anymore and o.k. if I'm all fucked up and, yes, every other race, creed & color sucks and the war in Nam is sanctioned by the Pope who is flawless of course and if I could just bend in half I could suck myself off all day and load up on some good scag and live in a closet because you can't beat them but you can ignore and induce ulcers and heart pangs and give them grey hair so to drive them stone bust on beauty parlor tint-up jobs and then you begin to cry in the closet because your veins are sore and you can't get over the fact that you love them somehow more or at least always.

The Basketball Diaries
by Jim Carroll

Memoir
M, 17
Winter, 1966
Seriocomic

A teenager Peeping Tom talks.

• • •

Smack across the alley from the back window of Headquarters, where I've been living these weekends, is this tall foxy chick's bedroom window in living color. Alley couldn't be more than six feet across and it seems she ain't found out yet about the shade being invented, so it's a show every morning her dressing for work and every night taking it off again. This does not include the many bonus hours on her days off bobbing around her big naked body past the window or right in front of the mirror playing around with her perfect spoons. Bitch is naked so much in fact that I been getting sick of her lately. She's been in front of that mirror so much that I feel like kicking her out and getting someone else to move in. Perhaps a redhead for a change. I almost feel guilty bringing a chick up to my place with her there all the time, like once I brought up this chick maybe a week ago and we're in bed and I look over my shoulder and there she is combing away in the raw and I wanted to get out of bed with the chick I'm with just to watch her. You must be thinking I should shout over to her or something but, shit that would be horrible, that would ruin the whole thing.

"Beginnings" by Pat Conroy from *Three Minutes or Less: Life Lessons from America's Greatest Writers*

Essay
M, 40+
Contemporary
Dramatic

A writer takes vengeance upon his abusive father.

• • •

The worst thing that happened: (…) a fight broke out between my mother and father when my sister had her birthday party, her ninth birthday party. I was eleven. A fight started. My role was to get the other six kids out of harm's way. So I rushed them out of the room. My second job was to get Mom away from Dad. I went roaring in. I was eleven. Dad could eat Ollie North for breakfast. I got between them. I looked over my head and saw the butcher knife (…). Blood got on me, my sister. Mom took us to Hot Shoppes and said she was going to leave Dad. She did not. What she did instead was wash my shirt and my sister's dress that had the blood of my father on it.

Later, when I asked my sister if it happened, she said no, it didn't happen. I said, why not? She said we didn't write it down. If it's going to be real, you got to write it down.(…)

My father made one mistake. He was raising an American novelist and an American poet—and we wrote it down.

"Big Boy" by Theresa M. Carilli

Short story
M, 60s
Contemporary
Dramatic

Umberto (alias Big Boy) is an Italian-American ex-prizefighter.

• • •

I met Joe Louis at the garden. He took a liking to me and I became his sparring partner for twenty-five bucks a day. Back in 1942, that was good money. Blacks and Italians. We're known to be good at two things, and the other one's fightin. One day Louis and I were sparring at Riverside Stadium in Washington D.C. In front of 15,000 people I threw a punch directly at Louis. The only thing he couldn't handle was a punch thrown directly at him. I was more surprised than he was. They took him to the hospital because they thought I broke his jaw. I became a big celebrity. (…)

But, I never was successful as a fighter. I never been successful at anything because I don't have no god damned guts and no luck either. (…) I hated fighting. Broke my nose five times. Lost up to eight pounds in a fight. Once I got knocked in the head so hard I didn't know where I was for three days. A friend led me around. I did learn a few things from boxing—you can do anything you want in this world because most everybody's so god damned stupid.

"The Black Cat" by Edgar Allan Poe

Short story
M, 20+
New England, 1843
Dramatic

The speaker reports a repulsive act committed in a drunken stupor.

• • •

One night, returning home, much intoxicated, from one of my haunts about town, I fancied that the cat avoided my presence. I seized him; when, in his fright at my violence, he inflicted a slight wound upon my hand with his teeth. The fury of a demon instantly possessed me. I knew myself no longer. My original soul seemed, at once, to take its flight from my body; and a more than fiendish malevolence, gin-nurtured, thrilled every fibre of my frame. I took from my waistcoat-pocket a penknife, opened it, grasped the poor beast by the throat, and deliberately cut one of its eyes from the socket! (...)

When reason returned with the morning—when I had slept off the fumes of the night's debauch—I experienced a sentiment half of horror, half of remorse, (...) but it was, at best, a feeble and equivocal feeling, (...) I again plunged into excess, and soon drowned in wine all memory of the deed.

In the meantime the cat slowly recovered. The socket of the lost eye presented, it is true, a frightful appearance, but he no longer appeared to suffer any pain. He went about the house as usual, but, as might be expected, fled in extreme terror at my approach. I had so much of my old heart left, as to be at first grieved by this evident dislike on the part of a creature which had once so loved me. But this feeling soon gave place to irritation. And then came, as if to my final and irrevocable overthrow, the spirit of PERVERSENESS.

"The Black Cat" by Edgar Allan Poe

Short story
M, 20+
New England, 1843
Dramatic

The speaker defends his own perversity.

• • •

[p]erverseness is one of the primitive impulses of the human heart
(...)

Who has not, a hundred times, found himself committing a vile or a
stupid action, for no other reason than because he knows he should
not? Have we not a perpetual inclination, in the teeth of our best
judgment, to violate that which is *Law*, merely because we understand it to be such? (...)

It was this unfathomable longing of the soul to *vex itself*—to offer
violence to its own nature—to do wrong for the wrong's sake
only—that urged me to continue and finally to consumate the injury
I had inflicted upon the unoffending brute. One morning, in cold
blood, I slipped a noose about its neck and hung it to the limb of a
tree—hung it *because* I knew that it had loved me, and *because* I
felt it had given me no reason of offence—hung it *because* I knew
that in so doing I was committing a sin—a deadly sin that would so
jeopardize my immortal soul as to place it—if such a thing were
possible—even beyond the reach of the infinite mercy of the Most
Merciful and Most Terrible God.

On the night of the day on which this most cruel deed was done, I
was aroused from sleep by the cry of fire. The curtains of my bed
were in flames. The whole house was blazing.

"Blood-Burning Moon" from *Cane* by Jean Toomer

Novel
M, 20s–30s
Cotton fields, Georgia, 1920
Dramatic

Tom, in love with Louisa, does not want to believe the rumors he's heard. Here, he professes his devotion, entreats and inquires.

• • •

[w]ords is like th spots on dice: no matter how y fumbles em, there's times when they jes wont come. I dunno why. Seems like th love I feels fo yo done stole m tongue. I got it now. Whee! Louisa, honey, I oughtnt tell y, I feel I oughtnt cause yo is young an goes t church an I has had other gals, but Louisa I sho do love y. Lil gal, Ise watched y from them first days when youall sat right here befo yo door befo th well an sang sometimes in a way that like t broke m heart. Ise carried y with me into th fields, day after day, an after that, and I sho can plow when yo is there, an I can pick cotton. Yassur! Come near beatin Barlo yesterday. I sho did. yassur! An next year if ole Stole'll trust me, I'll have a farm. My own. My bales will buy yo what y gets from white folks now. Silk stockings an purple dresses—course I dont believe what some folks been whisperin as t how y gets them things now. White folks always did do for niggers what they likes. An they jes cant help alikin yo, Louisa. Bob Stone likes y. Course he does. But not the way folks is awhisperin. Does he, hon?

"The Bohemian Girl" by Willa Cather

Short story
M, 20+
Nebraska, 1910s
Dramatic

Nils, a Nebraska pioneer, convinces Clara to run away with him.

• • •

You can't sit on the bank and think about it. You have to plunge. That's the way I've always done, and it's the right way for people like you and me. There's nothing so dangerous as sitting still. You've only got one life, one youth, and you can let it slip through your fingers if you want to; nothing easier. Most people do that. You'd be better off tramping the roads with me than you are here. (…)

But I'm not that kind of a tramp, Clara. You won't have to take in sewing. I'm with a Norwegian shipping line; came over on business with the New York offices, but now I'm going straight back to Bergen. I expect I've got as much money as the Ericsons. Father sent me a little to get started. They never knew about that. There, I hadn't meant to tell you; I wanted you to come on your own nerve.(…)

One has to tear loose. You're not needed here. Your father will understand; he's made like us. As for Olaf, Johanna will take better care of him than ever you could. It's now or never, Clara Vavrika. My bag's at the station; I smuggled it there yesterday. (…)

Where's your old dash, Clara Vavrika? What's become of your Bohemian blood? I used to think you had courage enough for anything. Where's your nerve—what are you waiting for?

"Boy Born with Tattoo of Elvis" from *Tabloid Dreams* by Robert Olen Butler

Short story
M, 16
Algiers, Louisiana. Contemporary
Seriocomic

A boy born with a tattoo of Elvis on his chest tells it like it is.

• • •

I carry him on my chest and it's a real tattoo and he was there like that when I come out of Mama. That was the week after he died, Elvis, and Mama made the mistake of letting folks know about it (...). It was just as well for her that most people didn't believe. She covered me up quick. Not more than one or two of her boyfriends ever knew—and there was many more than that come through in these sixteen years. The couple of them who saw me without my shirt and remarked on it thought she'd had it done to me, and she never said nothing about it being there when I was still inside her, and one of them got real jealous (...), thinking that she was so much in love with Elvis that she had him tattooed on her son and that meant she was probably thinking about the King when the boyfriend and her was thrashing around on her bed, and she never said nothing to make him think that wasn't so and he hit her and I just went out the door and off down the street to the river (...). You see, I'm not Elvis myself. I'm not him reincarnated as that one newspaper tried to make you believe. I didn't come out of my mama humming 'Heartbreak Hotel,' like they said.

"Canadians" from *Rule of the Bone* by Russell Banks

Novel
M,14
Au Sable, upstate New York, 1994.
Dramatic

Chappie—aka Bone—is an abused runaway. While hanging out in the local mall, he watches a younger girl in the company of an odd, older man who, Chappie suspects, is abusing her.

• • •

Basically people don't know how kids think, I guess they forget. But when you're a kid it's like you're wearing these binoculars strapped to your eyes and you can't see anything except what's in the dead center of the lenses because you're too scared of everything else or else you don't understand it and people expect you to, so you feel stupid all the time. Mostly a lot of stuff just doesn't get registered. You're always fucking up and there's a lot that you don't even see that people expect you to see, like the time after my thirteenth birthday when my grandmother asked me if I got the ten dollars and the birthday card she sent me. I said to her I don't know and she started dissing me to my mom and all. But it was true, I really didn't know. And I wasn't even into drugs then.(...)

The little girl in the red dress was wearing binoculars over her eyes like I did when I was her age and she couldn't see that she was in danger any more than I could have seen it back then, only it was different for her now because she had me to help her and I didn't have anyone.

"Cats and Students, Bubbles and Abysses" from *The Watch* by Rick Bass

Short story
M, 20s
Contemporary South
Seriocomic

A college student complains about his roommate.

• • •

I got a roommate, he's tall and skinny, when we get in arguments he says "I went to Millsaps," uses the word like what he thinks a battering ram sounds like. He's a real jerk, I could break both his arms just like that! if I wanted to, I've got a degree in English Literature from Jackson State, I was the only white on campus, I can't use "I went to Jackson State" like a battering ram, but I can break both his arms. (...)

I swear one of these days I'm gonna kill him, he may have gone to Millsaps ("'Saps," he calls it, there, you hate him too) but he doesn't know how to use a Kleenex. Instead he just goes around making these enormously tall wet sniffles, if you could hear just one of them you would first shiver and then you too would want to kill him. If they catch me and bring me to court I suppose I can always bring that up in the trial, I must go out and buy a tape recorder first thing tomorrow but first the cat needs feeding, he's a violent little sonuvabitch. (...)

His name is W. C. He's the only thing I like about Jackson, Mississippi. He's a bad-ass: he only eats live pigeons. You know how cats can be finicky.

"The Celebrated Jumping Frog of Calaveras County" by Samuel Longhorn Clemens

Short story
M, 50+
The dilapidated tavern in a decayed mining camp, 1865
Comic

The rotund and bald Simon Wheeler spins a yarn for an inquiring stranger.

• • •

Well, thish-yer Smiley had rat-tarriers, and chicken cocks, and tom-cats and all them kind of things, till you couldn't rest, and you couldn't fetch nothing for him to bet on but he'd match you. He ketched a frog one day, and took him home, and said he cal'lated to educate him; and so he never done nothing for three months but set in his back yard and learn that frog to jump. And you bet he *did* learn him, too. He'd give him a little punch behind, and the next minute you'd see that frog whirling in the air like a doughnut—see him turn one summerset, or maybe a couple, if he got a good start, and come down flat-footed and all right, like a cat. He got him up so in the matter of ketching flies, and kep' him in practice so con-stant, that he'd nail a fly every time as fur as he could see him. Smiley said all a frog wanted was an education, and he could do 'most anything—and I believe him. Why, I've seen him set Dan'l Webster down here on this floor—Dan'l Webster was the name of the frog—and sing out, "Flies, Dan'l, flies!" and quicker'n you could wink he'd spring straight up and snake a fly off'n the counter there, and flop down on the floor ag'in as solid as a gob of mud, and fall to scratching the side of his head with his hind foot as indifferent as if he hadn't no idea he'd been doin' any more'n any frog might do. You never see a frog so modest and straightfor'ard as he was, for all he was so gifted. And when it come to fair and square jumping on a dead level, he could get over more ground at one straddle than any animal of his breed you ever see. Jumping on a dead level was his strong suit, you understand; and when it come to that, Smiley would ante up money on him as long as he had a red. Smiley was monstrous proud of his frog, and well he might be, for fellers that had traveled and been everywheres, all said he laid over any frog that ever *they* see.

A Certain Age by Tama Janowitz

Novel
M, 40+
A New York cocktail party, contemporary
Comic

The wealthy Charlie Twigall—not the most stellar conversationalist—corners Florence Collins at a cocktail party.

• • •

I spent the day...trying to get them...to fix my car. (...) It's in a... garage...the dealership...out here. It still ...smells. They said...it was fixed...but when I went to the SAAB dealership...I said, 'I can still ...detect an odor.' And the salesman...the man who sold it to me ...initially...got in. And he said, 'I don't smell...anything.' I said, 'You must have an olfactory...problem.' (...)

I was extremely...angry...and I asked if he wouldn't mind...sitting in the car. After a few minutes...of sitting in the car...he said that they would try...again. (...) Meanwhile...I ordered a new Lotus...but it's on...back order for the summer. (...) I took Mother's...car and driver for the evening. Mother...gave up driving. She says...traffic these days. (...) When she first started...coming here...as a girl...it wasn't at all...fashionable. And it was...the country. In those days...it took five hours...to get to Southampton.(...) The roads...were single-lane ...or something. Now...it takes almost that long...because of the traffic. (...)

Do you want to...sit outside? It's so...nice out, and it might be... easier to talk.

"A Christmas Memory" by Truman Capote

Short story
M, 30+
Alabama, circa 1931
Dramatic

A young man fondly recalls a very special childhood friend.

• • •

A woman with shorn white hair is standing at the kitchen window. She is wearing tennis shoes and a shapeless gray sweater over a summery calico dress. She is small and sprightly, like a bantam hen; but, due to a long youthful illness, her shoulders are pitifully hunched. Her face is remarkable—not unlike Lincoln's, craggy like that, and tinted by sun and wind; but it is delicate too, finely boned, and her eyes are sherry-colored and timid. "Oh my," she exclaims, her breath smoking the windowpane, "It's fruitcake weather!" (...)

I am seven; she is sixty-something. We are cousins, very distant ones, and we have lived together—well, as long as I can remember. Other people inhabit the house, relatives; and though they have power over us, and frequently make us cry, we are not, on the whole, too much aware of them. We are each other's best friend. She calls me Buddy, in memory of a boy who was formerly her best friend. The other Buddy died in the 1880s, when she was still a child. She is still a child.

"I knew it before I got out of bed," (she says, turning away from the window...) "The courthouse bell sounded so cold and clear. And there were no birds singing; they've gone to warmer country, yes indeed. Oh, Buddy, stop stuffing biscuit and fetch our buggy. Help me find my hat. We've thirty cakes to bake."

A Crack-up at the Race Riots
by Harmony Korine

Novel
M, 20s
A prison, contemporary
Seriocomic

An imagined monologue spoken by slain rapper Tupac Shakur to a friend.

• • •

I been watchin' baseball on the set (I got the biggest TV you ever seen, the kinda boob that when we wuz children they didn't even have shit like this, a small movie screen with drink holders comin' out the side), an the Braves is slamin' this year, mad homers an a fly infield. When I was locked up you sent me music an I must tell you lil' homie that shit kept my ass in check, some jazz, some blues, an the rock shit was cool, The Who, I read the liner notes about Keith Moon and that shit struck me for some reason, I wrote a song based on his childhood called "The Boy Trapped in the Moon," the beat is funky, that nigga Dre Bone flew in the beats from his crills in Florida, we sampled a buncha shit from Marvin Gaye an this crazy slide guitar from a country album. I'm gonna tour a little bit with Snoop an some others but I'm gonna be out your way real soon so get ready. But listen yo I'm much calmer these days. I felt like I been seein' the light burn bright as hell an that shit singed my skin with the word Righteous, it don't mean I ain't no thugg, that as you know is my destiny, but the time is time an my ass is gonna sit back, rhyme, get hella busy with the bitches, keep prayin' day after day, buy shoes, whatever, the important thing is just livin' in step, the tragedy is yesterday's news homie, that shit is straight-up fin as they say in the French land.

"Cruising Paradise" from *Cruising Paradise: Tales by Sam Shepard* by Sam Shepard

Short story
M, 30+
Southwest, 1960s
Seriocomic

Sam Shepard narrates a teenage memory.

• • •

Crewlaw's dad had burned himself up in a motel bed. That was the story. Mattress exploded or something. The details kept bothering me. Crewlaw told me the cause of it was a bog cigar ember that had flopped off while his dad was unconscious; drunk. The ember had rolled down his T-shirt, found its way to the sheets, and burned clear through the mattress, causing internal combustion. I couldn't quite picture it, although Crewlaw related it as though he'd been a witness to the whole event. He got personally insulted that I wasn't getting it, and took the attitude that I thought he was lying to me, which I knew he wasn't. He said he'd take me over to the motel where it happened and show me the mattress itself, if I didn't believe him. I told him I *did* believe him, I just couldn't picture it, but he dragged me out there anyway. (…)

The death mattress was standing on its end, leaning against a porch railing with a giant black hole burned clear through to daylight. It looked like a bomb had dropped on it. Crewlaw pulled it away from the railing and stuck his whole arm through the hole so his hand came out the other side. He opened and closed his fist, grabbing at air. (…)

"Burnt clear through. See that? That's what a cigar can do. Now maybe you can picture it."

Dancer with Bruised Knees
by Lynne McFall

Novel
M, teens/20s
Contemporary
Dramatic

Sunny, a psychopath, comments on the sorry state of the world.

• • •

When I first got here I tried not to be an Ugly American. I kept my door closed, my legs covered, my voice down. (...)

Everyone told me that a year abroad would change my life, but I thought my transformation would come in the form of a tall, cool French woman who could lift one eyebrow to call a cab.

No.

I should say here that though I do not look at all French, people always stop me to ask directions (...). So, walking along the rue de Fleurus that day, I thought the three guys in the car were asking directions, and I turned around.

The one on the passenger side said, "Are you a homosexual?"(...). I didn't know much French then, but I could say "little frog," so I did: "No, but you can suck my dick anyway, *petite grenouille.*"

He became enraged—perhaps he knew more English than I gave him credit for— (...)

I put my backpack on the ground and calmy rummaged through it. When my attacker came bounding toward me I shot him, right between the eyes, with the pistol that I carry for such purposes. Then, because I'm not the kind of guy to leave things unfinished, I shot the other two, and took their leather jackets as trophies. Then I went to McDonald's.

O Mom. The world is ugly, and the people are sad.

"The Darling" by Anton Chekhov

Short story
M,30+
Russia, 1899
Seriocomic

Kukin, manager of an open-air theater, addresses Olenka, effectively his landlady and owner of the rooming house in which Kukin lives. He laments, then embraces, his own bad luck.

• • •

There! That's the life we lead, Olga Semyonova. It's enough to make one cry. One works and does one's utmost, one wears oneself out, getting no sleep at night, and racks one's brain what to do for the best. And then what happens? To begin with, one's public is ignorant, boorish. I give them the very best operetta, a dainty masque, first rate music-hall artists. But do you suppose that's what they want! They don't understand anything of that sort. They want a clown; what they ask for is vulgarity. And then look at the weather! Almost every evening it rains. It started on the tenth of May, and it's kept it up all May and June. It's simply awful! The public doesn't come, but I've to pay the rent just the same, and pay the artists. (...)

Well, rain away, then! Flood the garden, drown me! Damn my luck in this world and the next! Let the artists have me up! Send me to prison! To Siberia! the scaffold! Ha, ha, ha!

"The Death of Justina" from *The Stories of John Cheever* by John Cheever

Short story
M, 40s
Contemporary
Seriocomic

Moses explains why he has been particularly agitated of late.

• • •

On Saturday the doctor told me to stop smoking and drinking and I did. (…) I told my wife—when she passed through the living room—that I had stopped smoking and drinking but she didn't seem to care and who would reward me for my privations? Who cared about the bitter taste in my mouth and that my head seemed to be leaving my shoulders? (…) When it was time for us to go out I was so light-headed that I had to ask my wife to drive the car. On Sunday I sneaked seven cigarettes in various hiding places and drank two Martinis in the downstairs coat closet. At breakfast on Monday my English muffin stared up at me from the plate. I mean I saw a face there in the rough, toasted surface. The moment of recognition was fleeting, but it was deep, and I wondered who it had been. Was it a friend, an aunt, a sailor, a ski instructor, a bartender, or a conductor on a train? The smile faded off the muffin but it had been there for a second—the sense of a person, a life, a pure force of gentleness and censure—and I am convinced that the muffin had contained the presence of some spirit. As you can see, I was nervous.

Deliverance by James Dickey

Novel
M, 30s
The South, circa 1970
Dramatic

*Ed and his canoe-trip companions are being stalked by a
mountain man intent on killing them.*

• • •

The question is, what is *he* going to do? (...)

What can he lose now? He's got exactly the same thing going for
him that we had going for us when we buried his buddy back in
the woods. There won't be any witnesses. There's no motive to
trace him by. As far as anybody else knows, he's never seen us and
we've never seen him. If all four of us wind up in the river, that'll
just even things out. Who in the hell cares? What kind of a search
party could get up into these rapids? (...) You think anybody's going
to fly a helicopter down into this gorge, just on the chance that he
might see something? Not a chance in the world. (...)

We're caught in this gorge. He can't come down here, but the only
way out of this place for us is down the river. We can't run out of
here at night, and when we move in the morning he'll be up there
somewhere. (...)

Or somebody can try to go up there and wait for him on top. (...)
It's either him or us. We've killed a man. So has he. Whoever gets
out depends on who kills who. It's just that simple.

"A Dill Pickle" by Katherine Mansfield

Short story
M, 40/50
a city; 1920
Comic

*A middle-aged, would-be suitor scares off an old flame—
once again.*

• • •

What a marvellous listener you are. When you look at me with
those wild eyes I feel that I could tell you things that I would never
breathe to another human being. (...) Before I met you, I had never
spoken of myself to anybody. How well I remember one night, the
night that I brought you the little Christmas tree, telling you all
about my childhood. And of how I was so miserable that I ran away
and lived under a cart in our yard for two days without being discovered. And you listened, and your eyes shone, and I felt that you
had even made the little Christmas tree listen too, as in a fairy story
(...) It seems such ages ago. I cannot believe that it is only six years.
(...) I've often thought how I must have bored you. And now I
understand so perfectly why you wrote to me as you did—although
at the time that letter nearly finished my life. I found it again the
other day, and I couldn't help laughing as I read it. It was so
clever—such a true picture of me. (...)

Ah, no, please (...) don't go just for a moment (...) I see so few people to talk to nowadays, that I have turned into a sort of barbarian
(...) Have I said something to hurt you? (...)

What I really wanted then, (...) was to be a sort of carpet—to make
myself into a sort of carpet for you to walk on so that you need not
be hurt by the sharp stones and the mud that you hated so. It was
nothing more positive than that—nothing more selfish. Only I did
desire, eventually, to turn into a magic carpet and carry you away to
all those lands you longed to see (...)

I felt you were more lonely than anybody else in the world (...) and yet, perhaps, that you were the only person in the world who was really, truly alive. Born out of your time (...) Fated. (...)

And then the fact that you had no friends and never had made friends with people. How I understood that, for neither had I. Is it just the same now?

"Dog" from *Town Smokes* by Pinkney Benedict

Short story
M, teens
West Virginia, Contemporary
Seriocomic

Broom speculates on the nature of the dog beneath his trailer in West Virginia.

• • •

Did you hear that? (...)

I bet it's Seldomridge's dog (...). You know that big black bastard of a hound he got that's all the time getten in people's sheep. Somebody probably poisoned the son of a gun. (...)

I hope it ain' got the rabies (...). I seen a dog that had the rabies once and it is an awful thing. (...)

Got bit by a coon or a skunk and that sucker was plain crazy. Slobbers all over his mouth and blood runnen out his snout and down his chin. Walked all stiff-legged and hunchback and snapped at everthen that come too near. (...)

Ended up by finally tearen his own guts out, he was that out of his head. Nothen else to bite on so he ripped out his own belly and bleeden and howlen while he buried his nose. Jesus was that somethen. (...)

The county sheriff even come out to the trailer park where it was after a while but it was already dead by that time (...). Big fat deputy put a round into it jest to make sure but it was dead as hell, flies crawlen on its tongue and all. (...)

You see it? (...) I'd hate for that to be Seldomridge's big old dog under there and stinken with the rabies. He'd bite on you sure as hell and then you'd have it too. (...)

You see it yet?

Dog Day Afternoon by Patrick Mann

Novel
M, 20s–30s
Queens, early 1970s
Seriocomic

LittleJoe, a gay Vietnam vet, addresses one of his hostages during a Chase Bank heist.

• • •

Let's hear from you, Mr. Family Man. Any shouts of 'faggot' from you? (…)

I'm talking to you, Boyle (…). Now you know who heisted your precious little corner of Chase's precious little world. Two asshole bandits. Two father fuckers. And it's killing your Irish soul, isn't it (…) Mr. Guardian of Catholic Morality?

But I don't only hold the gun, I hold the cards, the whole fucking deck, Boyle. I'm like Superman. I can see through steel. I can see your little scummy office love affair, and that gives me more power than this thirty eight. I can tell Sam to wipe you out in the next five seconds and that would be it. But that's only life-and-death power. I also have the power to bad-name you till the end of time. I can hang a sign on your tombstone that will keep your wife and kids and mother and sisters and priest in tears forever. Adulterer. Christ, it's almost too good. What if that crowd out there wasn't yelling 'faggot' at the top of their lungs? What if they were yelling 'adulterer' at a good Catholic husband and father like you? (…)

Nobody'd yell anything like that (…). 'Adulterer' isn't a curse word. Only 'faggot' is.

Enduring Love by Ian McEwan

Novel
M, 30s
Contemporary England
Dramatic

*After witnessing a ballooning accident with Joe, Jed Parry
becomes obsessed with him, believing something special
has passed between them.*

• • •

When you came out of your house yesterday evening and you
brushed the top of the hedge with your hand, I didn't understand at
first. I went down the path and put out my own hand and fingered
the leaves that you had touched. I felt each one, and it was a shock
when I realized they were different from the ones you hadn't
touched. There was a glow, a kind of burning on my fingers along
the edges of those wet leaves. Then I got it. You had touched them
in a certain way, in a pattern that spelled a simple message. Did you
really think I would miss it? Joe! So simple, so clever, so loving.
What a fabulous way to hear of love, through rain and leaves and
skin, the pattern woven through the skein of God's sensuous cre-
ation unfolding in a scorching sense of touch. I could have stood
there for an hour in wonder, but I didn't want to be left behind. I
wanted to know where you were leading me through the rain. (...)

I hope it thrills you, the way it thrills me when you guide me with
your messages, these codes that tap straight into my soul. I know
that you'll come to God, just as I know that it's my purpose to bring
you there, through love. Or, to put it another way, I'm going to
mend your rift with God through the healing power of love.

Joe, Joe, Joe (...). I'll confess it, I covered five sheets of paper with
your name.

"Everything Is Green" from *Girl with Curious Hair* by David Foster Wallace

Short story
M, 48
A trailer in a trailer park, 1980s
Dramatic

Mitch pleads with Mayfly to talk with him.

• • •

Mayfly I can not feel what to do or say or believe you any more. But there is things I know. I know I am older and you are not. And I give to you all I got to give you, with my hands and my heart both. Every thing that is inside me I have gave you. I have been keeping it together and working steady every day. I have made you the reason I got for what I always do. I have tried to make a home to give to you, for you to be in, and for it to be nice. (...)

Mayfly my heart has been down the road and back for you but I am forty-eight years old. It is time I have got to not let things just carry me by any more. I got to use some time that is still mine to try to make everything feel right. I got to try to feel how I need to. In me there is needs which you can not even see any more, because there is too many needs in you that are in the way. (...)

[it] really does not matter what I seen or what I think I seen. That is not it any more. I know I am older and you are not. But now I am feeling like there is all of me going in to you and nothing of you is coming back any more.

"First Love" by Christopher Buckley from *Three Minutes or Less: Life Lessons from America's Greatest Writers*

Essay
M, 20+
Contemporary
Seriocomic

A man relates his first love—for a gun.

• • •

My first love was a gun. A Browning .22 semi-automatic rifle. I know. I know. (…)

Let me point out that this was not an assault weapon. This was the sort of rifle that hundreds of thousands of red-blooded American boys cut their teeth on without growing up to be disgruntled postal workers. I don't know why they're so disgruntled. We're the ones whose mail is always late. Anyway, from the moment I first saw it in the catalog of sports, it was love at first sight. (…) I begged and begged my father. (…) [f]inally he relented one birthday. I remembered great excitement when I saw on the box of cartridges that their range was one and a half miles. I vividly recall too the look on my father's face when I asked him how high the planes were that flew over the house on their way to land at LaGuardia Airport.

What a beautiful piece of work it was.

Fishboy by Mark Richard

Novel
M, 30s
Contemporary
Seriocomic

Aboard a trawler manned by a crew of renegades, John, "a tattooed giant," eulogizes their recently departed cook.

• • •

God, take from us the soul of this, your nearly split-in-two servant here, the Cook, and let him taste the Gruel and Slop of Everlasting Afterlife, that is, if he has indeed risen to serve in Your Galley, instead of broiling in Your Eternal Oven where his shipmate Lonny here who suffered his cooking thinks he deserves to go. (...)

And God, we are actually thankful for delivering us from his fare that gave us the shits, this cook's heart so small he cheated us at our rations, harboring that broken bag of lemon sours and that flask of lime juice when the scurvy was upon us, our gums bleeding and us swallowing our teeth; but most importantly we thank You for taking him so quickly so that he didn't suffer that much, really. (...)

You see, Lord, there is no meanness in how I just settle the folds in the funeral shroud with my foot here, and here, and here and STEP AWAY LONNY! I didn't mean to set a bad example! THAT'S ENOUGH KICKING! LEAVE OFF from kicking the carcass! I said. So God, take this very, very, lucky bastard from us and back into Your employ to serve up boot biscuits and snot-rag stew to Your Legion of Angels who always fail us, those bright-eyed nancies with mighty swords and lacy pants.

And one last thing (...). Help me keep my foot on the necks of these your serpents, servants.

And let me finally net my loved one. (...)

Amen.

"For Jeromé—With Love and Kisses" by Gordon Lish

Short story
M, 50+
Contemporary
Comic

A father lectures his son. Lish strings together clichés from the Jewish vernacular in this imagined monologue spoken by the father of J.D. Salinger.

• • •

Boychik, this is your father's advice to you from your father's heart of hearts. In words of one syllable, darling, there comes a time when you have to say to yourself enough is enough. But let's face it, who am I to open my mouth and try to teach a genius like yourself? Listen, just because I am the father and know from bitter experience, does this make me entitled to tell you what it's all about? Forget even that I am the elder, Jerome. Forget even that I as your father would jump off the highest building for you. It still doesn't give me the right to come along and spell out the facts of life for a person who is a genius, even if it just so happens he doesn't know which end is up.

But meanwhile, boychik, your father knows what he knows, and he didn't wait around for some professor to come along and spell out the facts of life. You name me the subject, Jerome, every college in the world will tell you there is one rule that is first and foremost, and for your information it's the one which says enough is definitely enough.

Freedomland by Richard Price

Novel
M, 30+
New Jersey, contemporary
Dramatic

*Lorenzo Council is an ambitious black detective in fictional
Dempsy, New Jersey. Brenda is the white victim of a high-
media car-jacking. Lorenzo has taken Brenda to a decrepit
theme park called Freedomtown to escape the media frenzy
and to try to get her to open up to him.*

• • •

You want to hear the best thing that ever happened to me out
here? The, the highlight of my teenage years? (…) I was here one
Saturday with these three friends from Armstrong? And Mary Wells
was up on that stage, you remember her? "The One Who Really
Loves You," "You Beat Me to the Punch," "Two Lovers"…Yeah, well
anyways, we were way up front by that stage there and she was
beautiful. To me, she was, oh man…And I was up there in front,
like, not even hearin' her, just lookin'…And she sees me, she's
smilin', singin', I go off in a daydream, you know, like when you're
kind of drivin' on a highway you just, like, go off? And next thing I
know somebody's pullin' on my wrist, and I thought someone was
messin' with me. I wasn't all there, but I look up and it's her…Mary.
And she's pullin' on me, trying to get me up on the goddamn stage
and I'm, like, Oh my God. She gets me up on the goddamn stage,
me and my fourteen-year-old ass, and like, I'm dreamin' this, I'm
dreamin' this. And she has me do a duet with her on 'Two Lovers,'
you remember that? (…)

I can't remember the rest, but, see, both lovers were the same guy
split into two, kind and loving, and the other person, when he was
treating her bad, messin' around on her, like, a split personality. But,
you know, I swear, the older I get the more I think that song is
about everybody, you know what I'm saying? How…I mean we're all
two people. Damn, some people I can think of are at least two people.

Geek Love by Katherine Dunn

Novel
M, 30s/40s
Contemporary
Seriocomic

Al Binewski, proprietor of a carnival family of freaks, tells his children, all proud freaks, of the first time he met their mother.

• • •

There I was, hosing the old chicken blood and feathers out of the geek pit on the morning of July 3rd and congratulating myself for having good geek posters, telling myself I was going to sell tickets by the bale (...) when up trips your mama, looking like angelfood, and tells me my geek has done a flit in the night, folded his rags as you might say, and hailed a taxi for the airport. (...)

I couldn't climb into the pit myself because I was doing twenty jobs already. Suddenly your mama pops up for all the world like she was offering me sherry and biscuits. 'I'll do it, Mr. Binewski,' she says, and I just about sent a present to my laundryman. (...)

She fluttered around like a dainty bird, and when she caught those ugly squawking hens you couldn't believe she'd actually do anything. When she went right ahead and geeked 'em that whole larruping crowd went bonzo wild. There never was such a snap and twist of the wrist, such a vampire flick of the jaws over a neck or such a champagne approach to the blood. She'd shake her star-white hair and the bitten-off chicken head would skew off into the corner while she dug her rosy little fingernails in and lifted the flopping, jittering carcass like a golden goblet, and sipped! (...) She was magnificent, a princess, a Cleopatra, an elfin queen! That was your mama in the geek pit.

"Halfway Home" by Paul Monette

Short story
M, 30s/40s
Contemporary
Dramatic

*A gay man with AIDS speaks to his homophobic brother
who has come to visit after many years of silence.*

• • •

You still a good Catholic? (…) According to them, I'm evil, you
know. That's the latest doctrine, from God's mouth to the Pope's
ear. "Intrinsic evil." (…) Maybe you guys get to wink at the priest
while you fuck your brains out. (…) But they're still beating up fags
in Chester, because Her Holiness says it's cool. (…) And sixty percent of the priests are fags anyway! (…)) They hate us for being
out. They liked it the old way, where you get to be special friends
with the altar boys, and maybe you cop a feel off little Jimmy
Murphy after Mass— (…)

Dad went to Mass every Sunday, too. (…) And you know what? He
was still a scumbag drunk who hit me for nothing at all. He used to
hit me for reading. And when I finally told him I was gay, he told
me I made him want to puke. (…) Isn't that where you learned it?
(…) So you'll forgive me if I keep my distance from all good
Catholics.

"Hard Sell" from *If the River Was Whiskey* by T. Coraghessan Boyle

Short story
M, 20s/30s
Tehran, 1988
Comic

*A hip image consultant discusses his first encounter with
the Ayatollah.*

• • •

So maybe I come on a little strong.

'Hey, babes,' I say to him (through his interpreter, of course, the guy
with a face like a thousand fists), 'the beard's got to go. And that
thing on your head too—I mean I can dig it and all; it's kinda wild,
actually—but if you want to play with the big boys, we'll get you a
toup.' I wait right there a minute to let the interpreter finish his jab-
bering, but there's no change in the old bird's face—(...) But what
the hey, I figure, he's paying me a hundred big ones up front, the
least I can do is give it a try. 'And this *jihad* shit, can it, will you? I
mean that kinda thing might go down over here, but on Santa
Monica Boulevard, believe me, it's strictly from hunger.'

Then the Ayatollah looks at me, one blink of these lizard eyes he's
got (...) and he says something in this throat-cancer rasp (...) and
the interpreter stands, the fourteen guys against the wall with Uzis
stand, some character out the window starts yodeling the midday
prayers, and I stand too. I can feel it, instinctively—I mean, I'm per-
ceptive, you know that, Bob—that's it for the first day. I mean,
nothing. Zero. Zilch (...). All these clowns with Uzis closing in on me
like piranha, and I'm thinking how in Christ does this guy expect to
upgrade his image when half the country's in their bathrobe morning, noon, and night?

Hard Times by Charles Dickens

Novel
M, 30s/40s
London, 1854
Dramatic

Mr. Thomas Gradgrind, a retired wholesale hardware merchant, explains his expectations to Mr. McChoakumchild, the schoolmaster he has just hired.

• • •

Now, what I want is Facts. Teach these boys and girls nothing but facts. Facts alone are wanted in life. Plant nothing else, and root out everything else. You can only form the minds of reasoning animals upon Facts: nothing else will ever be of any service to them. This is the principle on which I bring up my own children, and this is the principle on which I bring up these children. Stick to Facts, sir! (...)

You are to be in all things regulated and governed, (...) by fact. We hope to have, before long, a board of fact, composed of commissioners of fact, who will force the people to be a people of fact, and of nothing but fact. You must discard the word Fancy altogether. You have nothing to do with it. You are not to have, in any object of use or ornament, what would be a contradiction in fact. You don't walk upon flowers in fact; you cannot be allowed to walk upon flowers in carpets. You don't find that foreign birds and butterflies come and perch upon your crockery; you cannot be permited to paint foreign birds and butterflies upon your crockery. You never meet with quadrupeds going up and down walls; you must not have quadrupeds represented upon walls. You must see, (...) for all these purposes, combinations and modifications (in primary colours) of mathematical figures which are susceptible of proof and demonstration. This is the new discovery. This is fact. This is taste. (...)

Now, if Mr. McChoakumchild (...) will proceed to give his first lesson here (...)

Mr. McChoakumchild, we only wait for you.

"Here and There" from *Girl with Curious Hair* by David Foster Wallace

Short story
M, 20s
Rural Maine, present
Comic

Bruce has gone to stay with a favorite aunt and uncle in the wake of a painful breakup with his girlfriend. Here he offers insight into his relationship with his brother, Leonard.

• • •

I let my aunt do the talking to my parents. I do, though, have one odd and unsatisfactory phone conversation with my eldest brother, who is an ophthamologist in Dayton. He smokes a pipe and is named Leonard. Leonard is far and away my least favorite relative, and I have no clue why I call him one night, collect, very late, and give him an involved and scrupulously fair edition of the whole story. We end up arguing. Leonard maintains that I am just like our mother and suffer from an unhappy and basically silly desire to be perfect; I say that this has nothing constructive to do with anything I've said, and that furthermore I fail to see what's so bad about wishing to be perfect, since being perfect would be...well, perfect. Leonard invites me to think about how *boring* it would be to be perfect. I defer to Leonard's extensive and hard-earned knowledge about being boring, but do point out that since being boring is an imperfection, it would by definition be impossible for a perfect person to be boring. Leonard says I've always enjoyed playing games with words in order to dodge the real meanings of things; this segues with suspicious neatness into my intutitions about the impending death of lexical utterance, and I'm afraid I indulge myself for several minutes before I realize that one of us has severed the connection. I curse Leonard's pipe, and his wife with a face like the rind of a ham.

"Heroes" by Tim O'Brien from
Three Minutes or Less: Life Lessons from America's Greatest Writers

Essay
M, 40+
Contemporary
Dramatic

*A Vietnam veteran remembers a man he met while consid-
ering whether to dodge the draft.*

• • •

America gave me Vietnam. I spent twenty years giving it back. What
happened was this: When I got drafted, I decided to run away. I
lived in Minnesota, which is a state north of Mexico, adjacent to the
Canadian border. (…) So I packed a bag and I drove north to a river
called the Rainy River, which separates Minnesota from Canada. To
think things over for a while, I stopped at a fishing resort called the
Tip Top Lodge. (…) Elroy Birdall was the caretaker, and for six days
in the summer of 1968 Elroy watched over me as I made my decision. He asked no questions, but he knew there was a war on. He
knew that, he knew my age, he saw the terror in my eyes, he heard
me squealing in my sleep, he knew Canada was just a boat ride
away. Even so, he didn't press me, he offered no advice, he fed me
and gave me a place to lie low. (…) He was a witness, like God, or
like the gods who look on in absolute silence as we live our lives, as
we make our choices, or fail to make them. He was a hero. I wasn't.
I went to Vietnam.

"How to Tell a True War Story" from *The Things They Carried* by Tim O'Brien

Short story
M, 40s
Dramatic
Contemporary

O'Brien recounts an experience in Vietnam.

• • •

The dead guy's name was Curt Lemon. (...)

In the mountains that day, I watched Lemon turn sideways. He laughed and said something to Rat Kiley. Then he took a peculiar half step, moving from shade into bright sunlight, and the booby-trapped 105 round blew him into a tree. The parts were just hanging there, so Dave Jensen and I were ordered to shinny up and peel him off. I remember the white bone of an arm. I remember pieces of skin and something wet and yellow that must've been the intestines. The gore was horrible, and stays with me. But what wakes me up twenty years later is Dave Jensen singing "Lemon Tree" as we threw down the parts. (...)

Twenty years later, I can still see the sunlight on Lemon's face (...) But if I could ever get the story right, how the sun seemed to gather around him and pick him up and lift him high into a tree, if I could somehow recreate the fatal whiteness of that light, the quick glare, the obvious cause and effect, then you would believe the last thing Curt Lemon believed, which for him must've been the final truth. (...)

And in the end, of course, a true war story is never about war. It's about sunlight.

"I Want to Know Why"
by Sherwood Anderson

Short story
M, teens
Saratoga, New York, 1930s
Seriocomic

*A Kentucky native rides the freight train to New York state,
and the fabled Saratoga racetrack.*

• • •

I can't help it, I'm crazy about thoroughbred horses. I've always
been that way. When I was ten years old and saw I was growing to
be big and couldn't be a rider I was so sorry I nearly died. Harry
Hellinfinger in Beckersville, whose father is Postmaster, is grown up
and too lazy to work, but likes to stand around in the street and get
up jokes on boys like sending them to a hardward store for a gimlet
to bore square holes and other jokes like that. He played one on
me. He told me that if I would eat a half a cigar I would be stunted
and not grow any more and maybe could be a rider. I did it. When
father wasn't looking I took a cigar out of his pocket and gagged it
down some way. It made me awful sick and the doctor had to be
sent for, and then it did no good. I kept right on growing. It was a
joke. When I told what I had done and why most fathers would
have whipped me but mine didn't.

"If You Can Count the Number" by Anacreon, Translated by Bernard Knox

Poem
M, 30+
Ancient Greece
Comic

A man boasts of his love life.

• • •

If you can count the number
of the leaves on all the branches,
or if you can find the total
of the waves in all the oceans,
I'll appoint you sole recorder—
you can catalogue my love life.

Now for Athens, just to start with,
write down the number thirty
and fifteen more for completeness.
After that, for Corinth, check off
love affairs in runs, in series
(for that city's in Achaea
where the girls are always handsome.)
Then take down the score for Lesbos,
Moving on towards Ionia
Via Caria and Rhodos—
and the total now: two thousand.

What's the matter? Feeling dizzy?
Wait until I get to Syria,
to the yearning sighs of Egypt,
not to speak of Crete—the island
that has everything, where Eros

runs amok in all the cities.
And I will not even mention
love affairs beyond Gibraltar
and across the Indian border
in my amorous grand total.

Ivanhoe by Sir Walter Scott

Novel
M, 20s/30s
England, 1194
Dramatic

Ivanhoe defends "chivalry" to Rebecca, who wonders about all the killing and bravado.

• • •

Rebecca, (…) thou knowest not how impossible it is for one trained to actions of chivalry to remain passive as a priest, or a woman, when they are acting deeds of honor around him. The love of battle is the food upon which we live—the dust of the melée is the breath of our nostrils! We live not—we wish not to live longer than while we are victorious and renowned. Such, maiden, are the laws of chivalry to which we are sworn, and to which we offer all that we hold dear. (…)

By the soul of Hereward! (…) thou speakest, maiden, of thou knowest not what. Thou wouldst quench the pure light of chivalry, which alone distinguishes the noble from the base, the gentle knight from the churl and the savage; which rates our life far, far beneath the pitch of our honor; raises us victorious over pain, toil and suffering, and teaches us to fear no evil but disgrace. (…) Chivalry!—why maiden, she is the nurse of pure and high affection—the stay of the oppressed, the redresser of grievances, the curb of the power of the tyrant. Nobility were but an empty name without her, and liberty finds the best protection in her lance and her sword.

"Jackson Hole, Wyoming, October 1985" from *Do Not Go Gentle...* by Daniel L. Vice

Memoir
M, 32
Jackson Hole, Wyoming. October, 1985
Dramatic

Dan Vice died on July 27, 1999.

• • •

It is autumn. I have been transferred here with my airline job. Jackson Hole, Wyoming. Home of the Grand Tetons, gateway to Yellowstone National Park. (...) This is the season for the locals to wind down from the hectic summer rush, to relax, to regroup. This is their time to prepare for the long winter (...).

I have taken to spending my afternoons driving just north of town to the Elk Refuge. Thousands of elk come to this meadow for the annual rut. The elk remain here for winter and are fed. I can stand here for hours relaxing and watching these magnificent animals.

It is on one of these afternoon outings that I notice I have small pea-sized lumps on the back of my neck. I have been feeling (...) fatigued for a few weeks now.

So I go to see a doctor—I don't even remember his name. He sends me to the lab for an HTLV-3 test. (...)

I drive home in a trance. I run myself a bath, which is odd because I prefer showers. I soak and scrub myself for a long time. I get out, dry myself off and put on clean clothes.

I go to the Million Dollar Cowboy bar. I mount one of the bar stools, which is a saddle. I look into the mirror behind the bar and see the reflection of the real cowboys bending over the pool tables. I order ten, twelve, sixteen Miller Genuine Drafts. I don't remember leaving.

The next morning I wake up at home thinking—Yesterday didn't happen. I continue to tell myself—there was no test, or perhaps, I'll have another test later.

The next few weeks Jackson Hole, Wyoming remains quiet. The leaves of the aspen fall and the Grand Tetons become shrouded in clouds. The days become shorter and my long cold winter begins.

"Kabnis" from *Cane* by Jean Toomer

Novel
M, 30s/40s
Rural Georgia, 1920
Dramatic

*Ralph Kabnis, a teacher, has recently moved to rural
Georgia from the North.*

• • •

God Almightly, dear God, dear Jesus, do not torture me with beauty.
Take it away. Give me an ugly world. Ha, ugly. Stinking like
unwashed niggers. Dear Jesus, do not chain me to myself and set
these hills and valleys, heaving with folk-songs, so close to me that I
cannot reach them. There is a radiant beauty in the night that
touches and…tortures me. Ugh. Hell. Get up, you damn fool. Look
around. What's beautiful there? Hog pens and chicken yards. Dirty
red mud. Stinking outhouse. Whats beauty anyway but ugliness if it
hurts you? God, he doesn't exist, but nevertheless He is ugly. Hence,
what comes from him is ugly. Lynchers and business men, and that
cockroach Hanby, especially. How come that he gets to be principal
of a school? Of the school I'm driven to teach in? God's handiwork,
doubtless. God and Hanby, they belong together. Two godam
moral-spouters. Oh, no, I won't let that emotion come up in me.
Stay down. Stay down, I tell you. O Jesus, Thou art
beautiful…Come, Ralph, pull yourself together. Curses and adoration dont come from what is sane. This loneliness, dumbness, awful,
intangible oppression is enough to drive a man insane. Miles from
nowhere. A speck on a Georgia hillside. Jesus, can you imagine it—
an atom of dust in agony on a hillside? Thats a spectacle for you.
Come, Ralph, old man, pull yourself together.

Last Notes from Home
by Fred Exley

Novel
M, 30s–40s
A bar in Upstate New York, 1978
Seriocomic

Howie, his father, and Howie's buddy "Ex" are talking, and drinking, when the conversation turns to Howie's late, schizophrenic mother, Cookie. Here, Howie blows his stack.

• • •

I hate it when you do that to me, Pop. Use me for your straight man, your educated son from Colgate. I got a B.A. in business—with a C minus average, I might add—and learned more in a month working for you than I did in four years at Hamilton. I was a fucking jock, Pop. I don't give a goddamn if you do it in front of people we don't care about. But this is Ex, for Christ's sake. He's family, he was there at the beginning and don't think he can't see through that dumb wop facade of yours. It's humiliating, Pop. It's goddamn humiliating. (...)

It was the Silver Star, Pop. For Christ's sake, we're talking to Ex now. He knows what medals Bill won. (...turning back to Ex...) Pop always does that. As though the Silver Star wasn't good enough. Pop has to make it the Congressional. He does that with everybody he knows. Vince Lombardi never really cut me. I just decided because Pop was alone I'd come home and help him with business. Like you, Ex. You were only nominated for a National Book Award, right? Not when Pop tells it! *You won. You better goddamn well believe you won.* And Cookie, Mom, I should say. She was more beautiful than Elizabeth Taylor. And Cass was going to be even more beautiful than that!

Last Notes from Home
by Fred Exley

Novel
M, 40s
His bedroom, 3 A.M., 1978
Seriocomic

Fred has just been stabbed with a grilling fork, hurled by his beautiful girlfriend Robin, following a night of hard drinking.

• • •

It's Easter Sunday, Robin. Like Christ, I shall be resurrected by sunrise. Until then, I want to contemplate the—what is it you call it? Cosmos?—*cosmos* as fantasy. If, for example, Christ was into the fantasy—and I'm not saying he was—of being the son of God, does that negate the possibility that he was indeed the son of god? Moreover, who is the Jesus of Nazareth we fashion in our minds?— a secular, bearded, sweet-faced man—in Hollywood, ah, Hollywood, listen to this one, Robin, his armpits are hairless!—with a genius for metaphor, and doubtless the greatest gift for creating a personal mythology of anyone who ever walked the earth. And who are you and I, Robin, but a couple of unconscious worshipers who emulate Him with our every breath and gesture, you with your half-baked quackery about autumnal New England ancestors and Seven Sisters colleges and me with my own quackery of being a Novelist—should I capitalize Novelist?—when I know that my grasp of the metaphor is at best a paltry, pedestrian thing—yes, Robin, just a couple pathetic bohunks striving in our separate ways to create personal mythologies we deem worthy of us. (...)

Give me this night to myself, Robin, and I make you this promise. I shall never, never again condemn nor reprimand you for babbling out your fantasies for all the world to hear.

Leaving Las Vegas by John O'Brien

Novel
M, 30s
Contemporary
Dramatic

Ben is trying to commit suicide by drinking himself to death. He's just met Sera, a prostitute, and longs for a meaningful connection with her.

• • •

Don't run away! (...)

I came here hoping that I could find you again tonight. I can pay you if you want, but I'd rather just take you out as a friend. That is, I like you and would like to see you on a social basis, if you know what I mean. I don't know if you have a boyfriend, or for that matter, a girlfriend, but if you have some free time...maybe we could...have dinner. (...)

Sorry. My watch went the way of my car. I'm not only too drunk to drive anymore, but I'm also too drunk to participate in the world of timekeeping—even as an observer (...). See, in LA I kept running out of liquor after it was too late to go out and buy some. For some reason the clear-cut solution was to move someplace where it is never too late (...). Anyway, I was getting tired of being looked at funny when I would walk into a bar at six a.m. Even the bartenders in my neighborhood started preaching to me. Here people drink at all hours. No one cares. There may be legitimate reasons, vacations and whatnot, but it just doesn't matter because they're not from here. They're not overtly fucking up. (...)

I'm rambling. I really like you. You make me want to talk. I don't know what time it is.

Lenny by Valerie Kohler Smith

Novelization of a motion picture
M, 30s
New York, 1964
Dramatic

Lenny Bruce, a stand-up comic arrested numerous times for using foul language in nightclub routines, addresses a judge as he desperately defends himself in court at the end of his career. In the end, he is dragged away, still pleading.

• • •

If it please the court. I wish to defend myself. (...)

I don't believe I *should* lose here because I don't believe I'm doing anything wrong. (...) I mean, I believe I have the right to say the things I'm saying. (...)

Your Honor—if you'd just let me do my act for the court—I'll take my chances. If after you hear me do it, if you don't think it's funny—if it just strikes you as 'dirty' or 'obscene'— (...)

Look—I know you're a good person—and I—I mean it—I genuinely want your respect. Look, I know this legal system is the best in the world—but you can't *hear* me. (...)

Dontcha see, when I talk about 'Tits and Ass' I'm not up there just to shock the audience by repeating the words *tits* and *ass, tits* and *ass*—the point I'm trying to make your Honor, is that we live in a hypocritical society where— (...)

Your Honor—You're trying to stop the information! (...) See—That's where it's at, stopping the information. Well you can't—The information keeps the country strong. You need the deviate. Don't shut him up. The madman—You need him to stand up and tell you if you're blowing it. And the harder— (...) The harder you come down on him, the more you need him!

"The Lightning-Rod Man"
by Herman Melville

Short story
M, 20+
New England, 1854
Seriocomic

Traveling door-to-door during a thunderstorm, the
Lightning-Rod Man peddles his wares.

• • •

Tall men in a thunderstorm I avoid. Are you so grossly ignorant as
not to know, that the height of a six-footer is sufficient to discharge
an electric cloud upon him? Are not lonely Kentuckians, ploughing,
smit in the unfinished furrow? Nay, if the six-footer stand by running water, the cloud will sometimes *select* him as its conductor to
that running water. Hark! Sure, yon black pinnacle is split. Yes, a
man is a good conductor. The lightning goes through and through a
man, but only peels a tree. But sir, you have kept me so long
answering your questions, that I have not yet come to business. Will
you order one of my rods? (...) One rod will answer for a house so
small as this; look over these recommendations. Only one rod, sir;
cost, only twenty dollars. Hark! There go all the granite Taconics and
Hoosics dashed together like pebbles. By the sound, that must have
struck something. An elevation of five feet above the house, will
protect twenty feet radius all about the rod. Only twenty dollars,
sir—a dollar a foot. Hark!—Dreadful!—Will you order? Will you
buy? Shall I put down your name? Think of being a heap of charred
offal, like a haltered horse burnt in his stall; and all in one flash!

Love Medicine by **Louise Erdrich**

Novel
M, 20s
Ojibwe Reservation, 1980s
Seriocomic

Lipsha expresses strong feelings, including love and awe, for his grandparents.

• • •

I never really done much with my life, I suppose. I never had a television. Grandma Kashpaw had one inside her apartment at the Senior Citizens, so I used to go there and watch my favorite shows. For a while she used to call me the biggest waste on the reservation and hark back to how she saved me from my own mother, who wanted to tie me in a potato sack and throw me in a slough. Sure, I was grateful to Grandma Kashpaw for saving me like that, for raising me, but gratitude gets old. After a while, stale. I had to stop thanking her. One day I told her I had paid her back in full by staying at her beck and call. I'd do anything for Grandma. She knew that. Besides, I took care of Grandpa like nobody else could, on account of what a handful he'd gotten to be. (...)

[t]here is this woman here, Lulu Lamartine, who always had a thing for Grandpa. She loved him since she was a girl and always said he was a genius. Now she says that his mind got so full it exploded.

How can I doubt that? I know the feeling when your mental power builds up too far. I always used to say that's why the Indians got drunk. Even statistically we're the smartest people on the earth.

"Lyndon" from *Girl with Curious Hair* by David Foster Wallace

Short story
M, 40s
circa 1955
Seriocomic

Lyndon Baines Johnson, U.S. Senator from Texas, speaks with an applicant.

• • •

My name is Lyndon Baines Johnson. I own the fucking floor you stand on, boy. (...)

My name is Lyndon Baines *Johnson*, son. I am the Senator to the United States Senate from the state of Texas, U.S.A. I am the twenty-seventh richest personal man in the nation. I got the biggest wazoo in Washington and the wife with the prettiest name. So I don't care who your wife's Daddy knows—don't you slouch at this Senator, boy. (...)

"Every prospective part of the personnel in the office of the United States Senator from Texas shall be interviewed"—I'm reading this, boy, off this card here—"interviewed with the potential of being interviewed by any part of the personnel of the office he shall potentially work under." I wrote that. I don't care who your wife's Daddy's wife's internist knows—you're potentially under me, boy, and I'm interviewing you. What do you think of that? (...)

The president of this particular stretch of the Dirksen Building is me, Lyndon Johnson. And a president views, interviews, and reviews everything he presides over, if he's doing his job in the correct manner. (...)

Say, write that down for me, boy. (...) Plus "previews," (...) Stick in "previews" there at the start, son.

Maggie: A Girl of the Streets
by Stephen Crane

Novel
M, 20s
New York, 1890s
Seriocomic

Pete, a handsome and flashy bartender in the slums of New York, talks to his best friend Jimmy.

• • •

Dere was a mug come in deh place deh odder day wid an idear he wus goin' teh own deh place! Hully gee, he wus goin' teh own deh place! I see he had a still on an' I didn' wanna giv 'im no stuff, so I says: 'Git deh hell outa here an' don' make no trouble,' I says like dat! See? 'Git deh hell outa here an' don' make no trouble'; like dat. 'Git deh hell outa here,' I says. See?" (…)

Well, deh blokie he says: 'T'hell wid it! I ain' lookin' for no scrap,' he says (See?), 'but' he says, 'I'm 'spectable cit'zen an' I wanna drink an' purtydamnsoon, too.' See? 'Deh hell,' I says. Like dat! 'Deh hell,' I says. See? 'Don' make no trouble,' I says. Like dat. 'Don' make no trouble.' See? Den deh mug he squared off an' said he was fine as silk wid his dukes (See?) an' he wanned a drink damnquick. Dat's what he said. See?"(…)

Say, I jes' jumped deh bar an' deh way I plunked dat blokie was great. See? Dat's right! In deh jaw! See? Hully gee, he t'rowed a spittoon true deh front windee. Say, I taut I'd drop dead. But deh boss, he comes in after an' he says, 'Pete, yehs done jes' right! Yeh've gota keep order an' it's all right.' See? 'It's all right,' he says. Dat's what he said." (…)

The Man Who Loved Levittown
by W.D. Wetherell

Short story
M, 50+
Middle America, 1980s
Dramatic

Pushed to the snapping point because of all the changes taking place in his beloved suburban Levittown, Tom is driven to destroy the very thing he holds most dear.

• • •

I went out to the toolshed, took a five-gallon can of gasoline, went back inside (...), took off the cap, taped a piece of cheesecloth over the spout, went into the den.

Sprinkle, sprinkle. Right over the desk. Sprinkle (...). Then after that I went into the bathroom. I remembered redoing it with a bigger tub, new tiles, new cabinet. Sprinkle, sprinkle. Next I went up the stairs I'd built with Scotty from lumber we helped ourselves to at a construction project on the turnpike (...), up to the dormer I'd added on for the kids (...), thinking about the times I sat around the old DuMont watching Mickey Mouse Club with them waiting for Kathy to get home, almost made me stop right there.

I went downstairs, the can getting lighter, leaving a little trail behind me (...), into the twins' room where I sprinkled some on the curtains Kathy sewed, sprinkled some on the Davy Crockett hat Chris used to wear every time she came out of the bathtub (...). Sprinkle, sprinkle (...). Like watering plants. Like baptizing someone. The fumes getting pretty bad now. Sprinkle. Outside to the carport, over the beams, over the tools, over everything. Sprinkle, sprinkle. Splash.

And that's where I am right now. The carport (...)I'm going to wait until Silver gets home first. I want to make sure everyone on the block gets to see what $55,000, 32 years, looks like going up in smoke.

"The Mortal Immortal"
by Mary Shelley

Short story
M, 323 years old (but looks twenty)
England, July 16, 1833
Dramatic

Winzy has lived three hundred and three years after ingest-ing half a dram of an Elixir of Immortality he mistakenly believed would cure him "of love—of torture!"

• • •

Am I immortal? (...)

To have drained half the Elixir of Immortaility is but to be half immortal—my For-ever is thus truncated and null. (...) But again, who shall number the years of the half of eternity? I often try to imagine by what rule the infinite may be divided. Sometimes I fancy age advancing upon me. One gray hair I have found. Fool! do I lament? Yes, the fear of age and death often creeps coldly into my heart; and the more I live, the more I dread death, even while I abhor life. Such an enigma is man—born to perish—when he wars, as I do, against the established laws of his nature. (...)

I have gazed upon the blue depths of many a placid lake, and the tumultuous rushing of many a mighty river, and have said, peace inhabits those waters; yet I have turned my steps away, to live yet another day. I have asked myself whether suicide would be a crime in one to whom thus only the portals of the other world could be opened. I have done all, except presenting myself as a soldier or duellist, an object of destruction to my—no, NOT my fellow mortals, and therefore I have shrunk away. They are not my fellows. The inextinguishable power of life in my frame, and their ephemeral existence, place us wide as the poles asunder. I could not raise a hand against the meanest or the most powerful among them. Thus I have lived on for many a year—alone, and weary of myself— desirous of death, yet never dying—a mortal immortal. Neither ambition nor avarice can enter my mind, and the ardent love that gnaws at my heart, never to be returned—never to find an equal on which to expend itself—lives there only to torment me.

This very day I conceived a design by which I may end all—without self-slaughter, without making another man a Cain—an expedition, which mortal frame can never survive, even endued with the youth and strength that inhabits mine. Thus I shall put my immortality to the test, and rest for ever—or return, the wonder and benefactor of the human species.

The Mysteries of Pittsburgh
by Michael Chabon

Novel
M, 22
Contemporary
Seriocomic

After recently graduating from college, Art Bernstein discovers a complicated facet of love and sex.

• • •

We slept together. He would get up in the morning and rush off to work, scrabbling through piles of our mingled trousers and briefs, running his head under the sink, slamming the front door in farewell, and after he was gone I would spend the luxury of my extra hour by bathing in the (...) claw-foot tub and in the strangeness of it all. We lived well. Arthur cooked elaborate dinners (...). We sent our dirty clothes out to be cleaned and they came back as gifts, tied up in blue paper. And, as often as possible, we went to bed. I did not consider myself to be gay; I did not consider myself, as a rule. But all day long, from the white instant when I opened my eyes in the morning until my last black second of awareness of Arthur's fading breath against my shoulder, I was always nervous, full of energy, afraid. The city was new again, and newly dangerous, and I would walk its streets quickly, eyes averted from those of passersby, like a spy in the employ of lust and happiness, carrying the secret deep within me but always on the tip of my tongue.

"The New Lost Generation" by David Leavitt

Essay
M, 40s
Contemporary
Seriocomic

Leavitt reflects on his current work life, one "that makes a good biographical note in the back of a literary magazine— 'living and working in Manhattan'."

• • •

I used to think there was something gloriously romantic about the nine-to-five life. I used to imagine there could be no greater thrill than being part of the crush riding the escalator down from the Pan Am Building into Grand Central at 5:00. The big station ceiling, with its map of stars, would unfold about you, the escalator would slip down under your feet—you, so small, so anonymous in all that hugeness and strangeness. Yet you'd know you were different. Light on your feet at rush hour, you'd dodge and cut through the throng, find your way fast to the shuttle. (…)

Ha, as the old woman who has worked forty years in accounting says to everyone. Ha-ha.

It's 5:30. Outside the sun has set. Inside other people are still typing, still frenzied. Everyone works harder than you, no matter how hard you work. Everyone makes more than you do, no matter how much you make. You slip out silently, guilty to be leaving only a half hour late, wondering why you're not as ambitious as they are, why you don't have it in you to make it.

But when you get outside, the wind is cold on your face, the streets are full of people herding toward the subway. You put on your Walkman. You think that tonight you might like to go dancing. Then the Pointer Sisters come on, and you realize that, like John Travolta tripping down the streets of Brooklyn in Saturday Night Fever, you already are.

Night of Broken Souls
by Thomas Monteleone

Novel
M, 40s
Contemporary
Dramatic

A black cab driver from Manhattan undergoes hypnosis and remembers an experience from a previous life, in which he was a young Jewish boy captured by the Nazis during World War II.

• • •

A teenaged boy wearing a long gray scarf refuses to climb into the truck in front of us. He cries out that he will not go anywhere without his grandfather, who has fallen under the gate of the truck and now struggles to regain his footing. The *Schutzstaffel* soldiers on each side of the truck scream at the boy to be silent and move to the front of the truck. But the boy stands defiant and continues to cry out for his grandfather. An SS trooper moves quickly, thrusting his bayonet forward and up, so that it enters the boy's eye socket and exits the back of his skull. The other soldiers laugh and cheer as the boy momentarily dances on the end of the rifle like a hideous marionette, a galvanic response to sudden brain death. Another soldier drags the boy's horrified grandfather to his feet, shoves a Luger into the old man's mouth and pulls the trigger.

The spray of exploding tissue slaps me and Youssef across the face, we are so close. But I am afraid to wipe away the wet fragments of brain and scalp.

The soldier drops the old man's body to the roadway and exclaims loudly that the Jew-boy did not want to go anywhere without his grandfather. And now they are together, he says. All the soldiers laugh and applaud their appreciation of the soldier's wit. And the rest of us begin moving more quickly, more efficiently, into the trucks.

"Nobody Home" from *Rules of the Lake* by Irene Ziegler

Short story
M, 40s/50s
Central Florida, Contemporary
Dramatic

Edward Bartlett drives a fuel oil truck through his territory.

• • •

Big mess out on Kepler Road driving home from Andy's. Looked like a dog. Poor thing all tore up, guts spilled across the center line and the blood so black I thought it must be oil. I was in the fuel oil truck, and it was dark. I was going fast, too. I'm pretty sure it was a dog.

I got home, in spite of my blood alcohol level, which I work very hard at keeping elevated. The fine folks at Andy's Bar and Grill are usually obliging. You come home to an empty house, you need to have something to look forward to in the morning, even if it's only a hangover. Christ, listen to me. That's the beer talking. I got a job, a roof over my head and kids who call me on holidays. I'm doing all right.

Not like that dog. I wonder who hit that dog. Must have been tearing up the road to do what they did to that dog. Must have been a truck; trucks use Kepler Road to get to the interstate. I wonder if the guy driving that truck felt the dog roll beneath his wheels.

Nobody Thinks of Greenland
by John Griesemer

Novel
M, 40s+
Greenland, 1950s
Dramatic

*In a secret military hospital in Greenland during the Korean
War, General Vord explains to Rudy the realities of the
world engaged in a Cold War.*

• • •

Let me broaden your perspective a little (...) Let me talk to you
about security. About peace. About the way you learned to look at
the world. Think back. Picture the world map you used to look at in
your old schoolroom. Can you do that (...)? (...) You looked at that
map every day, no doubt. (...) It was how you came to know the
world. Sure, there might have been a globe in the class, but the
map hung there right before your eyes. Big. Bitter smelling when
you went right up to it and sniffed the ink. Painted on something
almost as heavy as oilcloth. The world. Part of your education. (...)
But you know, that map helped you get the world all wrong... It
was supposed to teach you about the world, but it gave the whole
wrong point of view. A totally erroneous perspective. See, it's the
Mercator projection. It screws up our outlook. It's got us believing
this hunk of rock and ice, this Greenland, is twice the size of the
United States of America. (...) You sit in your schoolroom, looking
up at the map over the blackboard, and Russia is over on the left
and the United States of America is over on the right. Or maybe
we're in the middle and Russia is split in half. At any rate, those
Mercator projections give you the idea the Russ lives in a land divided or, at the very least, on the far side of the known world from us,
and so we are safe. She's a distant land. Far off. She can't get us.
So, lullaby and good night... Well, that is one piece of class-A
foolishness.

Nobody Thinks of Greenland
by John Griesemer

Novel
M, 40s+
Greenland, 1950s
Dramatic

General Vord talks of the looming threat of the Atomic Age, and how defense against that threat conflicts with the protection of the dying soldiers in this hidden military hospital.

• • •

Polar ice... Zero protection in the Atomic Age against missiles. Even against bombers. And polar ice is all we've got between us and them. After these mountains, pal, it's all flat. Like flying across an empty plate. Of course, their missiles and bombers are easier to spot. They have no cover. But then, we have no protection. So, we need early warning, soldier. Because, mark my words, we're fighting the next one in the air. (...) The Russ has got sixteen major airfields on the Kola Peninsula alone. There are enough planes and firepower on that little spit of land to blow up the whole world. (...) But... Given the choice. (...) We need warning... We need to buy time. In an air war, time is measured in minutes to target, seconds to impact. The clock looms over schoolchildren under their desks, over citizens making it into bomb shelters. That's what this all comes down to. Early warning. Radar. (...) Good place, save for the local populace. (...) The Atomic Age is big... Bigger than me. Bigger than you. Bigger than these guys. They're already calling Korea the Forgotten War, and that stands to reason. You tend to forget plenty when something as big as the Bomb is looming, (...) something has to come first here. How do I take care of them and the defense of our country too? Of them and our whole God-blessed way of life?

"The Package Man" from *Cruising Paradise: Tales by Sam Shepard* by Sam Shepard

Short story
M, 40s
Contemporary Southwest
Seriocomic

A man in a bar toilet talks and talks before fatally shooting himself.

• • •

Package man. That's my game. I'm a package man. Total carcass. We use it all (...). Ground beef. Rib eyes. T-bones. Chops. Tenderloin. Entrails. Offal. We package the whole damn works.

Haven't been regular for three weeks now (...). Comes from liquor, I suppose. Only drink when I'm on the road. Which is most the time. Back home it's off-limits. Wife just laid down the law one day, and that's how it's been ever since. Can't say I mind actually. Gives me a chance to dry out now and then. Body needs that, I think. Otherwise it starts to putrefy. End up smellin' just like your old man. That's the scary part. I hate that. Start feelin' like yer livin' out some doomed past. Some destiny you've got no say in. Women are good that way, doncha think? Keep us on the straight and narrow. I've got the kids too. They help. They're good that way too. Responsibility never hurt a man. I miss that when I'm out here in the field. Responsibility. Course, you gotta go where the beef is. That's the long and short of it. Can't sit behind a desk somewhere and dream out the window. Gotta go right to the source of it.

"The Picture of Dorian Gray" by Oscar Wilde

Short story
M, 30+
England, 1890s
Comic

Lord Henry Wotton speaks to his friend Basil Hallward, the artist who has just completed a portrait of the handsome young Dorian Gray. Basil has refused to give the painting to Lord Wotton because he "has too much of himself in it."

• • •

Too much of yourself in it! Upon my word, Basil, I didn't know you were so vain; and I really can't see any resemblance between you, with your rugged strong face and your coal-black hair, and this young Adonis, who looks as if he was made out of ivory and rose-leaves. Why, my dear Basil, he is a Narcissus, and you— well, of course you have an intellectual expression and all that. But beauty, real beauty, ends where an intellectual expression begins. Intellect is in itself a mode of exaggeration, and destroys the harmony of any face. The moment one sits down to think, one becomes all nose, or all forehead, or something horrid. Look at the successful men in any of the learned professions. How perfectly hideous they are! Except, of course, in the Church. But then in the Church they don't think. A bishop keeps on saying at the age of eighty what he was told to say when he was a boy of eighteen, and as a natural consequence he always looks absolutely delightful. Your mysterious young friend, whose name you have never told me, but whose picture really fascinates me, never thinks. I feel quite sure of that. He is some brainless beautiful creature who should be always here in winter when we have no flowers to look at, and always here in summer when we want something to chill our intelligence. Don't flatter yourself, Basil: you are not in the least like him.

"The Picture of Dorian Gray" by Oscar Wilde

Short story
M, 30+
England, 1890s
Dramatic

Basil Hallward, an Oxford educated artist, explains to his friend Lord Harry Wotton his obsession with the handsome young Dorian Gray.

• • •

He is all my art to me now. (…) It is not merely that I paint from him, draw from him, sketch from him. Of course, I have done all that. But he is much more to me than a model or a sitter.

(…) In some curious way—I wonder will you understand me?—his personality has suggested to me an entirely new manner in art, an entirely new mode of style. I see things differently, I think of them differently. (…) The merely visible presence of this lad—for he seems to me little more than a lad, though he is really over twenty— his merely visible presence—ah! I wonder can you realize all that that means?

(…) Harry! if you only knew what Dorian Gray is to me! You remember that landscape of mine, for which Agnew offered me such a huge price but which I would not part with? It is one of the best things I have ever done. And why is it so? Because, while I was painting it, Dorian Gray sat beside me. Some subtle influence passed from him to me, and for the first time in my life I saw in the plain woodland the wonder I had always looked for and always missed.

Pink by Gus van Sant

Novel
M, 20s/30s
Contemporary
Comic

*A young director of television infomercials describes the
opening moments of a standard show.*

• • •

The lights are very bright. Everything has got to shine so that you
are literally burning your message into the viewer's retinas. (…)

We don't want to lose them in the beginning of the spot, so that's
why there is so much joy in the beginning like there is. We want our
viewers to be thinking: This is…uh…what the hell is this? So they
don't go changing the channel on you. (…)

All right, now, Felix is going to signal to the audience to quiet
down, because he is making it seem like he doesn't have much
time. This is a very important maneuver, because you want the
viewer to feel like the host of the show isn't going to waste his
time, so he has to look like he doesn't have much time either, which
is incorrect, because we have an entire thirty minutes, sometimes,
my God, an hour, to fill with practically nothing.

This "time" maneuver also is signaling to our home viewers that this
is going to be fast, and they are going to get what they are looking
for (they don't actually know what that is yet) soon, so they don't
have to worry about the channel changer, they are going to give
this kid a chance. This brings to mind one of the reasons that so
many of our informmercial presenters are teens. It's to play on the
sympathy of the older home viewers who hopefully are just beginning to think: Well, that's a nice boy, he could be ours.

Portrait of a Lady **by Henry James**

Novel
M, 30+
England, 1870s
Dramatic

*The wealthy, charming, and sophisticated Lord Warburten
professes his love for Isabel Archer. Lockleigh is Lord
Warburten's estate.*

• • •

One's right in such a matter is not measured by the time, Miss
Archer; it is measured by the feeling itself. If I were to wait three
months, it would make no difference; I shall not be more sure of
what I mean than I am today. Of course I have seen you very little;
but my impression dates from the very first hour we met. I lost no
time; I fell in love with you then. It was at first sight, as the novels
say; I know now that is not a fancy-phrase, and I shall think better
of novels forevermore. Those two days I spent here settled it; I don't
know whether you suspected I was doing so, but I paid—mentally
speaking, I mean—the greatest possible attention to you. Nothing
you said, nothing you did, was lost upon me. When you came to
Lockleigh the other day—or rather, when you went away—I was
perfectly sure. Nevertheless, I made up my mind to think it over, and
to question myself narrowly. I have done so; all these days I have
thought of nothing else. I don't make mistakes about such things; I
am a very judicious fellow. I don't go off easily, but when I am
touched, it's for life. It's for life, Miss Archer, it's for life.

The Prince of Tides **by Pat Conroy**

Novel
M, 40s
South Carolina, Contemporary
Dramatic

*The reminiscent adult narrator sets the scene for the rest of
the story.*

• • •

To describe our growing up in the low country of South Carolina, I
would have to take you to the marsh on a spring day, flush the
great blue heron from its silent occupation, scatter marsh hens as
we sink to our knees in mud, open you an oyster with a pocketknife
and feed it to you from the shell and say, "There. That taste. That's
the taste of my childhood." I would say, "Breathe deeply," and you
would breathe and remember that smell for the rest of your life, the
bold, fecund aroma of the tidal marsh, exquisite and sensual, the
smell of the South in heat, a smell like new milk, semen, and spilled
wine, all perfumed with seawater. My soul grazes like a lamb on the
beauty of indrawn tides. (...)

The truth is this: Things happened to my family, extraordinary
things. I know families who live out their entire destinies without a
single thing of interest happening to them. I have always envied
those families. The Wingo's were a family that fate tested a thousand times and left defenseless, humiliated, and dishonored. But my
family also carried some strengths into the fray, and these strengths
let almost all of us survive the descent of the Furies. Unless you
believe Savannah; it is her claim that no Wingo survived.

I will tell you my story.

Nothing is missing.

I promise you.

The Princess Bride: S. Morgenstern's Classic Tale of True Love and High Adventure by William Goldman

Novel
M, 30s/40s
Contemporary
Serio-Comic

This is one of the narrator's "interruptions" as he tells the story of The Princess Bride.

• • •

I was in my teens and there was this great woman who lived in my home town, Edith Neisser, dead now, and she wrote terrific books about how we screw up our children. I knew her 'cause her kid Ed got his haircuts from my pop (...) I was watching some kids play badminton and Ed had just shellacked me, and as I left the court for the porch, he said, "Don't worry, it'll all work out, you'll get me next time, and if you don't, you'll beat me at something else." Edith was reading this book and she didn't put it down when she said, "That's not necessarily true, you know."

I said, "How do you mean?"

And that's when she put her book down. And looked at me. And said it: "Life isn't fair, Bill. We tell our children that it is, but it's a terrible thing to do. It's not only a lie, it's a cruel lie. Life is not fair, and it never has been, and it's never going to be."

Would you believe that for me right then it was like one of those comic books where the light bulb goes on over Mandrake the Magician's head? (...)

Life isn't fair, and I'm telling you, one and all, you better believe it. I got a fat spoiled son (...). And he's always gonna be fat, even if he gets skinny he'll still be fat and he'll still be spoiled and life will never be enough to make him happy, and that's my fault maybe—make it all my fault, if you want—the point is, we're not created equal. I got a cold wife; she's brilliant, she's stimulating, she's terrific; there's no love; that's okay too, just so long as we don't keep expecting everything to somehow even out for us before we die.

Life isn't fair. It's just fairer than death, that's all.

"Put Yourself in My Shoes" from *Will You Please Be Quiet, Please?* by Raymond Carver

Short story
M, 40s
Contemporary
Seriocomic

Edgar Morgan accuses his guests (a writer named Myers and his wife) of breaching a lease agreement on a rented house.

• • •

Consider this for a possibility, Mr. Myers! (Morgan screamed.) Consider! A friend—let's call him Mr. X—is friends with…with Mr. and Mrs. Y, as well as Mr. and Mrs. Z. Mr. and Mrs. Y and Mr. and Mrs. Z do not know each other, unfortunately. I say unfortunately because if they had known each other this story would not exist because it would never have taken place. Now, Mr. X learns that Mr. and Mrs. Y are going to Germany for a year and need someone to occupy their house during the time they are gone. Mr. and Mrs. Z are looking for suitable accommodations, and Mr. X tells them he knows of just the place. But before Mr. X can put Mr. and Mrs. Z in touch with Mr. and Mrs. Y, the Ys have to leave sooner than expected. Mr. X, being a friend, is left to rent the house at his discretion to anyone, including Mr. and Mrs. Y—I mean Z. Now, Mr. and Mrs…Z move into the house and bring a cat with them that Mr. and Mrs. Y hear about later in a letter from Mr. X. Mr. and Mrs. Z bring a cat into the house even though the terms of the lease have expressly forbidden cats or other animals in the house because of Mrs. Y's asthma. The real story, Mr. Myers, lies in the situation I've just described. (…) That's the real story, Mr. Myers. (…) That's the real story that is waiting to be written.

Rambling Rose
by Calder Willingham

Novel
M, 35
Deep South, 1935
Seriocomic

Dave is Rose's new husband. Slightly drunk, and in a rage over her "ramblings," the following tops a list of complaints he has about being married to his young bride.

• • •

Well, this is a little embarrassin', Mrs. Hillyer, and I hope you don't mind if I speak to you about it. But...well, Rose is oversexed. It's a problem, and I think she'll always be like that, a leopard don't change its spots completely. To tell you the truth, real frankly, she ...well, she wants me to...she wants me to be a husband to her every night, and that's not natural (...). I spoke to Dr. Graves about it and he said once a week was natural (...).

Mrs. Hillyer, I'll...take her, excuse my sayin' it, and then go to sleep and the dern girl will wake me up at three in the morning' kissin' me. And that ain't all, next mornin' before I'm even woke up she's crawlin' all over me! That girl don't want to do it just once a day, she'd do it three or four times if I was able, and I'm not. A thing like that drains a man's nerves, it ain't healthy. She's oversexed, Mrs. Hillyer.

The Rapture of Canaan
by Sheri Reynolds

Novel
M, 50s/60s
Contemporary South
Dramatic

Herman Langston, founder and preacher of The Church of Fire and Brimstone and God's Almighty Baptizing Wind, speaks to his granddaughter, Ninah.

• • •

I don't ever want to hear you say something like that again. Do you understand me? *(He yelled.)* Your baby is *not* like Jesus. And I just pray to God that the rapture won't come until you get yourself straight with your maker, because if it does, you'll be left behind on this pitiful planet, left to have your limbs cut from your body by Satan's own army, but you won't die. I don't know how we failed you, but you've got to get your vision directed back on that cross. Because those soldiers will cut off your fingers and toes, one by one, and toss them into a great vat of boiling grease, and you'll hear them sizzle as they land there, but you won't die. They'll cut off your legs and your arms, and you won't be able to move, but you *won't die*. And the scorpions will stick their giant tails into your body, will rape you with their stingers, and you'll wish you could die, but you won't.

But Ninah, my child, if you'll just repent. If you'll just admit that you sinned and that James sinned, and that the awful burden of that sinfulness caused him to leave this life, then you can go to Heaven with us all. It won't be long, Ninah, before Christ returns for his bride. For the Bible says that he'll come in the blinking of an eye, and if your heart's not ready, they'll be no hope for your soul, no salvation when the moon meets the sun.

"Red Rover" from *Rule of the Bone* by Russell Banks

Novel
M, 14
AuSable, upstate New York, 1994
Dramatic

Chappie questions his mother, insisting she make a choice.

• • •

You know what, Mom? You wanna know what? I'll tell you what. *You* should choose. Yeah, you should choose between me and Ken! That's right, choose which one of us you want. 'Cause you can't have both. That's the one thing I can guarantee. So c'mon, Mom, choose one or the other. Ken or me. Let's get serious. (...)

Who d'ya want standing there beside you, Mom? Is it gonna be your stupid sicko drunk of a pervert of a husband, or the homeless boy who's your own flesh-and-blood son? Red Rover, Red Rover, who're you calling over, Mom? Is it me or is it Ken? (...)

[w]e used to play Red Rover and the teachers thought it was cute and all but it was scary, two line of kids holding hands facing each other across a distance and the one in the middle says, Red Rover, Red Rover, let Chappie come over, and I'd get all excited like I'd been chosen for something special. I'd let go of the hand of the kid on either side of me and I'd step out there in like no-man's-land between the two lines all alone and exposed and everyone looking at me and I'd wind up and start running straight at the line opposite as fast as I could. (...) I was secretly glad to be captured. I never wanted to be the big tough kid who ended up on the other side all by myself (...)

So who's it gonna be, Mom? The terrific husband or the terrible son?

Remains of the Day
by Kazuo Ishiguro

Novel
M, 60s
England, 1956
Dramatic

*Stevens is an idealistic and self-deceived English butler who
resolutely upholds British manners, while closing his eyes to
the politics of his employer Lord Darlington. Here he reflects
upon his three decades of service.*

• • •

Since my new employer Mr Farraday arrived, I've tried very hard,
very hard indeed, to provide the sort of service I would like him to
have. I've tried and tried, but whatever I do I find I am far from
reaching the standards I once set myself. (…) I've given what I had
to give. I gave it all to Lord Darlington. (…)

Lord Darlington wasn't a bad man. He wasn't a bad man at all. And
at least he had the privilege of being able to say at the end of his
life that he made his own mistakes. His lordship was a courageous
man. He chose a certain path in life, it proved to be a misguided
one, but there, he chose it, he can say that at least. As for myself, I
cannot even claim that. You see, I trusted. I trusted his lordship's
wisdom. All those years I served him, I trusted I was doing something worthwhile. I can't even say I made my own mistakes.
Really—one has to ask oneself—what dignity is there in that? (…)

I'm so sorry, this is so unseemly. I suspect I'm over-tired. I've been
travelling rather a lot, you see.

A River Runs through It
by Norman Maclean

Novel
M, 60+
Montana, 1970s
Dramatic

Now elderly, Norman Maclean remembers his boyhood in Montana, and the river that ran through his life.

• • •

It was here, while waiting for my brother, that I started this story, although, of course, at the time I did not know that stories of life are often more like rivers than books. (...)

Of course, now I am too old to be much of a fisherman, and now of course I usually fish the big waters alone, although some friends think I shouldn't. Like many fly fishermen in western Montana where the summer days are almost Arctic in length, I often do not start fishing until the cool of the evening. Then in the Arctic half-light of the canyon, all existence fades to a being with my soul and memories and the sounds of the Big Blackfoot River and four-count rhythm and the hope that fish will rise.

Eventually, all things merge into one, and a river runs through it. The river was cut by the worlds' great flood and runs over rocks from the basement of time. On some of the rocks are timeless rain-drops. Under the rocks are the words, and some of the words are theirs.

I am haunted by waters.

Rivethead by Ben Hamper

Memoir
M, 40s
Flint, Michigan, 1970s
Seriocomic

*Hamper worked on the assembly line as a riveter at GM's
Flint, Michigan, truck and bus plant for several years during
the 1970s.* Rivethead *chronicles that experience.*

• • •

Dead Rock Stars are singin' for me and the boys on the Rivet Line
tonight. Hendrix. Morrison. Zeppelin. The Dead Rock Star catalogue
churnin' outta Hogjaw's homemade boom box. There's Joplin and
Brian Jones and plenty of Lynyrd Skynyrd (...) The Dead Rock Stars
yowling at us as we kick out the quota. (…)

We're all here. Department 07, Blazer/Suburban Line—factory out-
post FF-15 stenciled in black spray paint on the big iron girder
behind Dougie's workbench. We're building expensive trucks for the
General Motors Corp. (...) As for the popularity of the Dead Rock
Stars on the Rivet Line, I've settled upon this private theory. The
music (...) is redundant and completely predictable. We've heard
their songs a million times over. In this way, the music of the Dead
Rock Stars infinitely mirrors the drudgery of our assembly jobs. Since
assembly labor is only a basic extension of high school humdrum, it
only stands to reason that the same wearied hepsters who used to
dodge economics class for a smoke in the boys' room would later in
life become fossilized to the hibernatin' soundtracks of their own
implacable youth. Let the eggheads in economics have David Byrne
and Laurie Anderson. The rivetheads be needin' their "Purple Haze"
and "Free Bird" just like tomorrow needs today.

The Satires of Juvenal
by Decimus Junius Juvenal,
translated by Rolfe Humphries

Epic poem
M, 60+
Ancient Rome, circa 60 A.D.
Seriocomic

*Umbricus, an old Roman, tells a friend why he is leaving
Rome, moving to "the ghost town of Cumae."*

• • •

(...)Since there's no place in the city, (...)
For an honest man, and no reward for his labors,
Since I have less today than yesterday, since by tomorrow
That will have dwindled still more, I have made my decision. I'm
      going
To the place where, I've heard, Daedalus put off his wings,
While my white hair is still new, my old age in the prime of its
      straightness,
While my fate spinner still has yarn on her spool, while I'm able
Still to support myself on two good legs, without crutches.
Rome, good-bye! Let the rest stay in the town if they want to, (...)

What should I do in Rome? I am no good at lying.
If a book's bad, I can't praise it, or go around ordering copies.
I don't know the stars; I can't hire out as assassin
When some young man wants his father knocked off for a price; I
      have never
Studied the guts of frogs, and plenty of others know better
How to convey to a bride the gifts of the first man she cheats with.
I am no lookout for thieves, so I cannot expect a commission
On some governor's staff. I'm a useless corpse, or a cripple.
Who has a pull these days, except your yes men and stooges
With blackmail in their hearts, yet smart enought to keep silent?
(...) Never let the gold of the Tagus,

Rolling under its shade, become so important, so precious
You have to lie awake, take bribes that you'll have to surrender,
Tossing in gloom, a threat to your mighty patron forever.

"Say Never" from *Girl with Curious Hair* by David Foster Wallace

Short story
M, 70s
A tenement apartment. Contemporary
Seriocomic

Labov, an elderly widower and retired tailor, describes his strong suit.

• • •

A thing that is no fun? *Stomach trouble.* You don't believe me, you ask Mrs. Tagus here, she'll illuminate issues. Me: no stomach trouble. A stomach of hardy elements, such as stone. Arthritis yes, stomach trouble no.

The tea is not helping Mrs. Tagus's stomach trouble. "Such discomfort Mr. Labov!" she says to me in my kitchen of my apartment, where we are. "Excuse me for the constant complaining, " she says, "but it seems that to me anything that is the least little worry these days means the automatic making of my stomach into a fist!" (...) She is making an example of a fist in the air in a firm manner I envy, because of the arthritis I have in my limbs every day, especially in these winters; but I only express sympathy to the stomach of Mrs. Tagus, who has been my best and closest friend since my late wife and then her late husband passed away inside three months of each other seven years ago may they rest in peace.

I am a tailor. Labov the North-side tailor who can make anything. Now retired. I chose, cut, fit, stitched and tailored the raccoon coat Mrs. Tagus has been wearing for years now and is now in my kitchen which my landlord keeps cold, like the rest of this apartment, which my late wife Sandra Labov and I first rented in the years of President Truman. The landlord wants Labov out so he can raise rent to a younger person. But he should know who should know better than a tailor how it's no trouble to wear finely stitched coats and wait for spring. An ability to wait has always been one of my abilities.

"Shelter" from *A Relative Stranger* by Charles Baxter

Short story
M, 25+
Contemporary
Dramatic

Cooper, a baker who volunteers at a local shelter for the homeless, has, on a whim, brought Billy Bell, a recent arrival at the shelter, home with him. Here, Billy responds to Cooper's wife's question "What makes you happy, Mr. Bell?"

• • •

I didn't have any dreams until today, (...) but now I do, seeing your cute house and your cute family. Here's what I'd like to do. I want to be *just like all of you.* I'd put on a chef's hat and stand outside in my apron like one of those assholes you see in the Sunday magazine section with a spatula in his hand, and, like, I'll be flipping hamburgers and telling my kids to keep their hands out of the chive dip and go run in the sprinkler or do some shit like that. I'll belong to do-good groups like Save the Rainforests, and I'll ask my wife how she likes her meat, rare or well-done, and she'll say well-done with that pretty smile she has, and that's how I'll do it. A wonderfull fucking barbecue, this is, with folding aluminum chairs and paper plates and ketchup all over the goddamn place. Oceans of vodka and floods of beer. Oh, and we've sprayed the yard with that big spray that kills anything that moves, and all the flies and mosquitoes and bunnies are dead at our feet. Talk about the good life. That has got to be it.

Snow Falling on Cedars
by David Guterson

Novel
M, 20s/30s
Puget Sound, 1954
Dramatic

Ishmael pleads with his childhood lover, Hatsue, a Japanese woman now married to a Japanese man, to ease his loneliness like she used to do before the war came between them.

• • •

I'm like a dying person (...). I haven't been happy for a single moment since the day you left for Manzanar. It's like carrying a weight around in my gut, a ball of lead or something. Do you know how that feels, Hatsue? Sometimes I think I'm going to go crazy, end up in the hospital in Bellingham. I'm crazy, I don't sleep, I'm up all night. It never leaves me alone, this feeling. Sometimes I don't think I can stand it. I tell myself this can't go on, but it goes on anyway. There isn't anything I can do. (...)

You'll think this is crazy (...). But all I want is to hold you. All I want is just to hold you once and smell your hair, Hatsue. I think after that I'll be better. (...)

I know you're married (...). I want to forget about you, I do. I think if you hold me I can start, Hatsue. Hold me once, and I'll walk away and never speak to you again.

I'm not talking about love (...). I'm not asking you to try to love me. But just as one human being to another, just because I'm miserable and don't know where to turn, I just need to be in your arms.

"So Much Water So Close to Home" from *Where I'm Calling From* by Raymond Carver

Short story
M, 30s
Contemporary
Dramatic

To his wife, Dean defends his decision not to interrupt his fishing trip even though he and his buddies had discovered a corpse close to their secluded spot.

• • •

What are you staring at me for? (...)

Tell me what I did wrong and I'll listen! It's not fair. She was dead, wasn't she? There were other men there beside me. We talked it over and we all decided. We'd only just got there. We'd walked for hours. We couldn't just turn around, we were five miles from the car. It was opening day. What the hell, I don't see anything wrong. No, I don't. And don't look at me that way, do you hear? I won't have you passing judgment on me. Not you. (...)

What do I know, Claire? Tell me. Tell me what I know. I don't know anything except one thing: you hadn't better get worked up over this (...) She was dead, dead, dead, do you hear?(...) It's a damn shame, I agree. She was a young girl and it's a shame, and I'm sorry, as sorry as anyone else, but she was dead, Claire, dead. Now let's leave it alone. Please, Claire. Let's leave it alone now.

Something Happened by Joseph Heller

Novel
M, 40s
Connecticut, early 1970s
Dramatic

Bob Slocum gets uncomfortably honest about his feelings for his mentally challenged son.

• • •

It is not true that retarded (brain-damaged, idiot, feeble-minded, emotionally disturbed, autistic) children are the necessary favorites of their parents or that they are always uncommonly beautiful and lovable, for Derek, our youngest child, is not especially good-looking, and we do not love him at all. We would prefer not to think about him. We don't want to talk about him. (...)

I've got to get rid of him and don't know how. And there's no one I can ask. There's no one I can tell I even want to, not even my wife, who wants to get rid of him also (but doesn't dare say so to me). Especially not my wife. We blame each other for him, when we aren't blaming ourselves, and that's another thing we haven't been able to say to each other yet.

"It's your fault, not mine." (...)

He does not seem to be mine. He may be my wife's. There is no idiocy in my family that I know of (or in hers). My wife has begged me not to use that word (which may be why I do. She winces every time.) (...)

Poor little brain-damaged tyke. No one is on your side.

"Song of Myself" by Walt Whitman

Poem
M, 37
America, 1850s
Dramatic

Whitman sees the grass as signifying the cycle of life—
death and rebirth—and more.

• • •

A child said What is the grass? fetching it to me with full hands,
How could I answer the child? I do not know what it is any more
   than he.

I guess it must be the flag of my disposition, out of hopeful green
   stuff woven.

(...)

And now it seems to me the beautiful uncut hair of graves.

Tenderly will I use you curling grass,
It may be you transpire from the breasts of young men,
It may be if I had known them I would have loved them,
It may be you are from old people, or from offspring taken soon
   out of their mothers' laps,
And here you are the mothers' laps.

This grass is very dark to be from the white heads of old mothers,
Darker than the colorless beards of old men,
Dark to come from under the faint red roofs of mouths.

(...)

What do you think has become of the young and old men?
And what do you think has become of the women and children?
They are alive and well somewhere,

The smallest sprout shows there is really no death,
And if ever there was it led forward life, and does not wait at the
  end to arrest it,
And ceas'd the moment life appear'd.

All goes onward and outward, nothing collapses,
And to die is different from what any one supposed, and luckier.

"Sonnet CXXXVIII" by William Shakespeare

Poem
M, 50+
England, 1600s
Seriocomic

A lover flatters his beloved with innocent lies.

• • •

When my love swears that she is made of truth
I do believe her, though I know she lies,
That she might think me some untutor'd youth,
Unlearned in the world's false subtleties.
Thus vainly thinking that she thinks me young,
Although she knows my days are past the best,
Simply I credit her false-speaking tongue:
On both sides thus is simple truth suppress'd.
But wherefore says she not she is unjust?
And wherefore say I not that I am old?
O, love's best habit is in seeming trust,
An age in love loves not to have years told:
　Therefore I lie with her and she with me,
　And in our faults by lies we flatter'd be.

"Sonny's Blues" from *Going to Meet the Man* by James Baldwin

Short story
M, 20s/30s
Harlem, 1950s
Dramatic

A young man explains to his older brother "what happened" when he was addicted to drugs, how the addiction is always with him, and how it relates to his life as a blues pianist.

• • •

It's terrible sometimes, inside, (…) that's what's the trouble. You walk these streets, black and funky and cold, and there's not really a living ass to talk to, and there's nothing shaking, and there's no way of getting it out—that storm inside. You can't talk it and you can't make love with it, and when you finally try to get with it and play it, you realize nobody's listening. So you've got to listen. You got to find a way to listen.

(And then he walked away from the window and sat on the sofa again, as though all the wind had suddenly been knocked out of him.) Sometimes you'll do anything to play, even cut your mother's throat. *(He laughed.)* Or your brother's. *(He sobered.)* Or your own. (…) Don't worry. I'm all right now and I think I'll be all right. But I can't forget—where I've been. I don't mean just the physical place I've been, I mean where I've been. And what I've been.

(…) I've been something I didn't recognize, didn't know I could be. Didn't know anybody could be. (…) It can come again (he said almost as though speaking to himself…) It can come again. (…) I just want you to know that.

"The Spread of Peace" from
How I Came West and Why I Stayed
by Alison Baker

Short story
M, 70s
A beach in Miami, 1980s
Seriocomic

*Here, intending to comfort, Harry speaks with Heather, a
young wife from Utah attending a convention without her
spouse, a stranger who has just blurted to Harry that she
"has cancer."*

• • •

It just so happens that I know something about lumps in the breast.
My wife never touched her own breasts; the thought of it made her
faint. Imagine! (...) Breasts were made to be covered up. Not like
today; they don't cover anything. So our son marries a nurse, and
what's the first thing she says to my wife? Touch yourself, she says.
Every month, you got to examine your breasts or you'll die.

Letty doesn't want her in the house. 'Don't bring her here,' she tells
him, but he don't listen; he's a good boy. Next thing you know,
Toni, that's her name—an Italian Catholic which let me tell you
doesn't go over big either—Toni brings over this box of fake breasts.
Falsies! Letty could of died. She won't look anyplace but out the
window. So Toni shows me how to do it. Palpate the tissue, check
out the nodes. Quadrant by quadrant. Feel this. Feel that. (...)

It's a new age, (...) sitting there with your daughter-in-law telling
you how to feel up imitation breasts while your wife looks out the
window. But here's the thing. There was five of them, all different
shapes and sizes, and they had different lumps. (...) All different. I
don't know if you know this, but some women's breasts are always
lumpy. All the time. Cystic. Nothing wrong with them; they're just
full of little knots. Perfectly healthy. You got breasts like that?

"Spunk" by Zora Neale Hurston

Short story
M, 30–50s
Florida, 1927
Seriocomic

Elijah Mosley, drinking Sass'prilla on the store porch with Walter Thomas, swaps gossip about Lena's first—and second—late husbands.

• • •

Aw, Ah doan know. You never kin tell. He might turn him up an' spank him fur gettin' in the way, but Spunk wouldn't shoot no unarmed man. Dat razor he carried outa heah ain't gonna run Spunk down an' cut him, an' Joe ain't got the nerve to go to Spunk with it knowing he totes that Army .45. He makes that break outa heah to bluff us. He's gonna hide that razor behind the first palmetto root an' sneak back home to bed. Don't tell me nothin' 'bout that rabbit-foot colored man. Didn't he meet Spunk an' Lena face to face one day las' week an' mumble sumthin' to Spunk 'bout lettin' his wife alone? (...)

You wrong theah, Walter. Tain't 'cause Joe's timid at all, it's 'cause Spunk wants Lena. If Joe was a passel of wile cats Spunk would tackle the job just the same. He's go after *anything* he wanted the same way. (...) He tole Joe right to his face that Lena was his. 'Call her and see if she'll come. A woman knows her boss an' she answers when he calls.' 'Lena, ain't I yo' husband?'

Joe sorter whines out. Lena looked at him real disgusted but she don't answer and she don't move outa her tracks. The Spunk reaches out an' takes hold of her arm an' says: 'Lena, youse mine. From now on Ah works for you an' fights for you an' Ah never wants you to look to nobody for a crumb of bread, a stitch of close or a shingle to go over yo' head, but me long as Ah live. Ah'll git the lumber for owah house tomorrow. Go home an git yo' things together! (...) Lena looked up at him with her eyes so full of love that they wuz

runnin' over, an' Spunk seen it an' Joe seen it too, and his lip started to tremblin' and his Adam's apple was galloping up and down
his neck like a race horse. Ah bet he's wore out half a dozen Adam's
apples since Spunk's been on the job with Lena. That's all he'll do.
He'll be back heah after while swallowin' an' workin' his lips like he
wants to say somethin' an' can't.

Tales of the City by Armistead Maupin

Novel
M, 30s
San Francisco, 1970s
Seriocomic

Brian, an out-of-work ex-lawyer, shares a joint with his neighbor Mary Ann and tells her about an unpleasant party he's attended.

• • •

A house party at Stinson Beach. (…) Picture this, O.K.? Five young married couples and me. Well …semi-young. Thirty to thirty-five. Still in Topsiders, mind you, but driving an Audi now and sending a couple of rug rats to the French-American School and swapping notes on their Cuisinarts …(…) Next image: a beach full of pink people, the women on one side, chattering about hot tubs and cellulite and the best place for runny Brie …and the guys out by the vollyball net, huffing and puffing in twelve-year-old Madras bermudas their wives have let out at least twice …and all these yellow-haired kids fighting over who gets to play with Big Bird and G. I. Joe… (…)

So here's our hero, in the middle of all this…wondering if he can get food stamps if he quits at Perry's…hoping to hell the Clap Clinic doesn't call this week… (…) And then this guy runs out of the house with his guitar slung around his neck like some refugee from Hootenanny, only he's a lawyer, right?…and he drops down in the sand and starts singing "I don't give a damn about a greenback dollar"…and everybody claps along and sings and jiggles kids in their laps…(…) Christ! I went back to the house when the singalong started and sat in an empty bedroom and smoked a joint and thanked my fucking lucky stars I wasn't trapped in that pathetic, middle-class prison!

The Talented Mr. Ripley
by Patricia Highsmith

Novel
M, 20s
Italy, 1950s
Seriocomic

*In an attempt to endear himself to Dickie Greenleaf, the
charming Tom Ripley confesses how he came to find Dickie
in Italy.*

• • •

I think I ought to tell you something else . . . Your father sent me
over here especially to ask you to come home. (…) He approached
me in a bar in New York …I told him I wasn't a close friend of
yours, but he insisted I could help if I came over. I told him I'd try.
(…)

I don't want you to think I'm someone who tried to take advantage
of your father …I expect to find a job somewhere in Europe soon,
and I'll be able to pay him back my passage money eventually. (…)

I can do a number of things—valeting, baby-sitting, accounting—
I've got an unfortunate talent for figures. No matter how drunk I
get, I can always tell when a waiter's cheating me on a bill. I can
forge a signature, fly a helicopter, handle dice, impersonate practically anybody, cook—and do a one-man show in a nightclub in case
the regular entertainer's sick. Shall I go on?

"The Tell-Tale Heart"
by Edgar Allan Poe

Short story
M, 20s
New England, 1843
Dramatic

Boasting of effective execution, a murderer recounts his motive, and method.

• • •

Object there was none. Passion there was none. I loved the old man. He had never wronged me. He had never given me insult. For his gold I had no desire. I think it was his eye! yes, it was this! One of his eyes resembled that of a vulture—a pale blue eye, with a film over it. Whenever it fell upon me, my blood ran cold; and so by degrees—very gradually—I made up my mind to take the life of the old man, and thus rid myself of the eye for ever.

Now this is the point. You fancy me mad. Madmen know nothing. But you should have seen *me.* You should have seen how wisely I proceeded—with what caution—with what foresight—with what dissimulation I went to work!

I was never kinder to the old man than during the whole week before I killed him. And every night, about midnight, I turned the latch of his door and opened it—oh, so gently! And then, when I had made an opening sufficient for my head, I put in a dark lantern, all closed, closed, so that no light shone out, and then I thrust in my head.(...) It took me an hour to place my whole head within the opening so far that I could see him as he lay upon his bed. Ha! — would a madman have been so wise as this? And then, (...) I undid the lantern cautiously—oh, so cautiously—(for the hinges creaked)—I undid it just so much that a single thin ray fell upon the vulture eye. And this I did for seven long nights—every night just at midnight—but I found the eye always closed; so it was impossible to do the work; for it was not the old man who vexed me, but his Evil Eye.

"That Spot" from *The Call of the Wild* by Jack London

Short story
M, 20+
The Yukon, 1898
Seriocomic

A sled dog that won't work confounds its "master."

• • •

There we were. Spring was on and we had to wait for the river to break. We got pretty thin before we decided to eat the dogs, and we decided to eat Spot first. Do you know what that dog did? He sneaked. How how did he know our minds were made up to eat him? We sat up nights laying for him, but he never came back, and we ate the other dogs. We ate the whole team.

And now for the sequel. You know what it is when a big river breaks up and a few billion tons of ice go out, jamming and milling and grinding. Just in the thick of it, (...) we sighted Spot (...) he didn't have a chance in a million. He didn't have any chance at all. After the ice run, we got into a canoe and paddled down to the Yukon, and down the Yukon to Dawson, (...) And as we came into the bank at Dawson, there sat that Spot, waiting for us, his ears pricked up, his tail wagging, (...)

The more I think of that Spot, the more I am convinced there are things in this world that go beyond science. On no scientific grounds can that Spot be explained. (...) The Klondike is a good country. I might have been there yet, and become a millionaire, if it hadn't been for Spot. He got on my nerves. I stood him for two years all together, and then I guess my stamina broke. It was the summer of 1899 when I pulled out. I didn't say anything to Steve. I just sneaked.

This Boy's Life by Tobias Wolff

Memoir
M, 40s
Washington State, 1950s
Seriocomic

*When his stepson gets beat up at school, Dwight takes
sadistic pleasure in telling him how he used to handle bul-
lies.*

• • •

When I was your age (...), there was a kid who used to sit behind
me in school and lip off all the time (...). Well, he lipped off just
once too often and I told him to shut up. (...)

Well, after school that day he waits across the street with this friend
of his and as soon as I come out of the building he yells something.
I guess he thought I was just going to go home and forget about it.
But I'll tell you something. With people like that, you've got to hurt
them, you've got to inflict pain. It's the only thing they understand.
Otherwise you've got them on your back for good. Believe me, I'm
speaking from experience.

Okay (...). There were these frozen horse turds lying all over the
place (...). So I picked one up and went over to this guy, but not acting tough, okay? *Not acting tough.* Acting more like, Oh gee, I'm so
scared, please don't hurt me. (...)

He of course starts in on me again, blah blah blah, and while he's
got his mouth open *I jam a road apple into it!* You should've seen
the look on his face. Then I hit the sucker in the breadbasket, and
down he goes. I sit on him for a while and hold my hand over his
mouth until the road apple starts melting, then I get up and leave
him there. I caught holy hell for it later on, but so what.

"Untitled" from *The Poems of Catullus* by Catullus, translated by Charles Martin

Poem
M, 20+
Ancient Rome
Comic

Catullus bargains for a free meal.

• • •

You will dine well with me, my dear Fabullus,
in a few days or so, the gods permitting.
—Provided you provide the many-splendored
feast, and invite your fair-complected lady,
your wine, your salt & all the entertainment!
Which is to say, my dear, if you bring dinner
you will dine well, for these days your Catullus
finds that his purse is only full of cobwebs.
But in return, you'll have from me Love's Essence,
—or what (if anything) is more delicious:
I'll let you sniff a certain charming fragrance
Which Venuses & Cupids gave my lady;
One whiff of it, Fabullus, and you'll beg the
Gods to transform you into a nose, completely!

"Untitled" from *Greek Lyrics* by Theognis, translated by Richmond Lattimore

Poem
M, 30+
Ancient Greece
Dramatic

A disappointed lover speaks to his young man, Kyrnos.

• • •

See, I have given you wings on which to hover uplifted
      high above earth entire and the great waste of the sea
without strain. Wherever men meet in festivals, as men
      gather, you will be there, your name will be spoken again
as the young singers, with the flutes clear piping beside them,
      make you into a part of the winsome verses, and sing
of you. And even after you pass to the gloom and the secret
      chambers of sorrow, Death's house hidden under the ground,
even in death your memory shall not pass, and it shall not
      die, but always, a name and a song in the minds of men,
Kyrnos, you shall outrange the land of Greece and the islands,
      cross the upheaving sea where the fish swarm, carried not
astride the back of a horse, but the shining gifts of the
      dark-wreathed
      Muses shall be the force that carries you on your way.
For all wherever song is you shall be there for the singers.
      So long as earth endures and sun endures, you shall be.
I did this. But you give me not the smallest attention.
      You put me off with deceits as if I were a little child.

Up from Slavery: An Autobiography by Booker T. Washington

Memoir
M, 40+
Year: 1901
Dramatic

Raised in slavery, Washington relates memories from his youth.

• • •

I cannot remember a single instance during my childhood or early boyhood when our entire family sat down to the table together, and God's blessing was asked, and the family ate a meal in a civilized manner. On the plantation in Virginia, and even later, meals were gotten by the children very much as dumb animals get theirs. It was a piece of bread here and a scrap of meat there. It was a cup of milk at one time and some potatoes at another. Sometimes a portion of our family would eat out of the skillet or pot, while some one else would eat from a tin plate held on the knees, and often using nothing but the hands with which to hold the food. When I had grown to sufficient size, I was required to go to the "big house" at meal-times to fan the flies from the table by means of a large set of paper fans operated by a pulley. Naturally much of the conversation of the white people turned upon the subject of freedom and the war, and I absorbed a good deal of it. I remember that at one time I saw two of my young mistresses and some lady visitors eating ginger-cakes, in the yard. At that time those cakes seemed to me to be absolutely the most tempting and desirable things that I had ever seen; and I then and there resolved that, if I ever got free, the height of my ambition would be reached if I could get to the point where I could secure and eat ginger-cakes in the way that I saw those ladies doing.

What's Eating Gilbert Grape?
by Peter Hedges

Novel
M, 30s
Contemporary Iowa
Seriocomic

Mr. Carter, who deprives his wife emotionally, complains to eighteen-year-old Gilbert about her.

• • •

Women, Gilbert. I'm married to a woman (...). And God knows I love her—God knows it. And we have two boys, but you knew that. And Todd and Doug—they are at church camp and they miss their parents, their house, and I thought when we picked them up, you know, today—this afternoon—I thought we'd bring them a reminder. Something that states our love without saying it. So my wife—God love her—this afternoon something happened to my wife—do you know what ? (...)

Well, my wife sets out to make a batch of cookies for my boys. It seems to me these cookies were the perfect gift. How many mothers make cookies for their kids? Not many these days. There was a time when all mothers did was make cookies. I am married to an exceptional woman. But sometimes, Gilbert, sometimes I wish I was somebody else's husband because sometimes...My wife...

My wife. Burns. A batch of cookies. It is no big deal. A disappointment for the boys, sure. But it is no big deal! Now she is crying like her life is destroyed, crying over a bad batch of cookies. Sometimes, I tell you, honestly, sometimes I want to put her head in the oven and turn on the gas.(...)

Oh God. I can't believe I just said that. Can you? I did not mean that about the oven. I can't believe I just said that.

"Wipeout" from *The Pugilist at Rest* by Thom Jones

Short story
M, 20s/30s
Contemporary
Seriocomic

The narrator, an expensive dresser and self-ordained lady-killer, discloses a few of his secrets.

• • •

I believe in the philosophy of rock 'n' roll. Like, "If you want to be happy for the rest of your life, don't make a pretty woman your wife." I mean, who can refute that? Can Immanuel Kant refute that? How can you refute that? I mean, really. Any guy knows this is true, even a shallow, superficial guy like me. Of course, I think almost all women are pretty. You have to make them feel special, make them have the best day of their life, and what woman doesn't look good on the best day of her life? (...)

You have to make them come to you and you just can't get emotionally involved. I mean, it's her ball game when you do that, when you start having pet names, knowing one another's favorite color, and she starts springing little anniversaries on you. The next thing you know, you're a daddy, with all that responsibility. You have to play that noninvolvement theme, and work that. Give them a little James Dean or Montgomery Clift or a little Rudolph Valentino action, and when they know they can't own you, they want you all the more and you're the victor. It's very simple. It's just a matter of style.

The Word on the Street
by Marcus Laffey

Essay
M, 30+
New York, contemporary
Dramatic

A New York cop grills Anna, a heroin dealer, and tries to get her to give up information about her provider, J.J.

• • •

Anna, there's only one way you can make this go away. You know that, right? It's through us, right? Talking, helping us out? It's not through J.J. We know him, too, and know you work for him. Today, he was hanging on the corner while you were running your ass ragged taking money and handing out bags of dope. And you're in cuffs and he's home, watchin' *Oprah*. Yeah, Anna, it's four o'clock already! You moved a couple hundred decks this morning for J.J.— ten bucks each, that's a couple grand. How much did he pay you, fifty bucks? Or did he just throw you a couple of bags for yourself? Is he gonna send a lawyer down for you, is he gonna water your plants while you're away?

"X" from *Strangers in Paradise* by Lee K. Abbot

Novel
M, 40s
New Mexico, contemporary
Seriocomic

Hobey Don Baker, Jr., a mathematics teacher and JV football coach relates a teenage memory of his father's anger.

• • •

...Another time, while I was doing the dishes—just had the glassware left, in fact—he wandered past me, whistling the tune he always used when the world worked right ("I'm an Old Cowhand"), and flung open the refrigerator. It was nearly seven, I guess, and he was about to have his after-dinner rum concoction. (...)

The freezer door went bang, and instantly he was at my elbow, breathing in a panic, hunched over and peering into my dishwater as if what lay at the bottom was sin itself. "What the hell are you doing?" he hollered. I went loose in the knees and he swept me out of the way. "How many times I got to tell you," he shouted, "glasses first—water's hottest and cleanest—then the flatware, plates, serving dishes. Save your goddam saucepans for last!"

I was watching the world turn black and trying to remember how to defend myself. (...)

Not only did he rewash all the dishes, but he also—now muttering about the loss of common sense—opened every cabinet, drawer and cupboard we have so he could spend the next five hours washing, in water so hot we were in danger of steamburn, every item in the house associated with preparing, serving and consuming food. Chafing dish, tureen, pressure cooker, double boiler, candy dish, meat thermometer, basting brush, strainer, lobster hammer—everything disappeared into his soapy water.

"The Year of Getting to Know Us" from *Emperor of the Air* by Ethan Canin

Short story
M, 32
Contemporary
Dramatic

A man remembers a significant day with his father.

• • •

On a Sunday afternoon when I was sixteen I went out to the garage with a plan my mother had given me.

I stepped into the trunk [of my father's car](...). I lay down, and then I reached up, slammed down the trunk, and was in the dark. (...) "Dad's rides," my mother had said to me the night before, "would be a good way for him to get to know you." It was the first week of the year of getting to know us better. (...)

"If he won't let you come," she said, "sneak along."

On the freeway (...), we made a sharp right onto gravel and pulled over and stopped.

My father opened the door (...). Then the passenger door opened (...). If I heard her voice today, twenty-six years later, I would recognize it.

"Angel," she said.

I heard the weight of their bodies sliding across the back seat, first hers, then his. They weren't three feet away (...). As I lay there, I went over the voice again in my head: it was nobody I knew. I heard a laugh from her, and then something low from him. (...)

"Dad," I whispered. Then rocking (...), my father's sudden panting, harder, and harder, his half-words. The car shook violently. "Dad," I whispered. I shouted, "Dad!"

His steps kicked up gravel. I heard jingling metal (...). He was standing over me in an explosion of light. (...)

He rubbed his hands down the front of his shirt. (...)

"What the goddamn," [he said.]

"You I Have No Distance From" from *Cruising Paradise: Tales by Sam Shepard* by Sam Shepard

Short story
M, 40s
Written May 15, 1995 from Scottsville, Virginia
Dramatic

The narrator measures love in terms of distance.

• • •

I can't remember what it was like before I met you. Was I always like this? I remember myself lost. I know that for sure. Wandering. Moving from one wild woman to the next. Staying, sometimes, just long enough to understand that their bewilderment was more pronounced than mine. At least that's the way they put it across. But I can't remember being this nervous before; this frazzled. I'd watch them from a distance: taking stoned sponge baths in their sinks; shaving black hash balls with razor blades; moving like slow-motion queens. Then they'd change into backyard girls from long ago, giggling and tucking their long legs up under themselves: the way they'd plunk down on their soft heels and then toss their hair like horses switch their tails.

But you I have no distance from. Every move you make feels like I'm traveling in your skin; every glance you take out the window, as though you were completely alone and dreaming in some other time. It does no good to wave my arms. Now everything's reversed.

Male or Female
Monologues

"Etiology" from *Girl, Interrupted* by Susanna Kaysen

Memoir
F/M, 18+
Contemporary
Dramatic

A former mental patient tells all.

• • •

This person is (pick one):

1. on a perilous journey from which we can learn much when he or she returns;

2. possessed by (pick one):
   a) the gods,
   b) God (that is, a prophet),
   c) some bad spirits, demons, or devils,
   d) the Devil;

3. a witch;

4. bewitched (variant of 2);

5. bad, and must be isolated and punished;

6. ill, and must be isolated and treated by (pick one):
   a) purging and leeches,
   b) removing the uterus if the person has one,
   c) electric shock to the brain,
   d) cold sheets wrapped tight around the body,
   e) Thorazine or Stelazine;

7. ill, and must spend the next seven years talking about it;

8. a victim of society's low tolerance for deviant behavior;

9. sane in an insane world;

10. on a perilous journey from which he or she may never return.

"Invitation" from *Where the Sidewalk Ends* by Shel Silverstein

Poem
F/M, 20s
Contemporary
Seriocomic

The speaker extends an invitation.

• • •

If you are a dreamer, come in,
If you are a dreamer, a wisher, a liar,
A hope-er, a pray-er, a magic bean buyer...
If you're a pretender, come sit by my fire
For we have some flax-golden tales to spin.
Come in!
Come in!

"Sonnet CXLVIII"
by William Shakespeare

Poem
F/M, 20+
England, 1600s
Dramatic

A lover debates whether love is blind.

• • •

O me, what eyes hath Love put in my head,
Which have no correspondence with true sight!
Or, if they have, where is my judgment fled,
That censures falsely what they see aright?
If that be fair whereon my false eyes dote,
What means the world to say it is not so?
If it be not, then love doth well denote
Love's eye is not so true as all men's 'No.'
How can it? O, how can Love's eye be true,
That is so vex'd with watching and with tears?
No marvel then, though I mistake my view;
The sun itself sees not till heaven clears.
O cunning Love! with tears thou keep'st me blind,
 Lest eyes well-seeing thy foul faults should find.

The Wind in the Willows
by Kenneth Grahame

Novel
F/M, 20+
England, circa 1899
Comic

Rat scolds his friend Toad for bad behavior.

• • •

Now, Toady, I don't want to give you pain, after all you've been through already, but seriously, don't you see what an awful ass you've been making of yourself? On your own admission you have been handcuffed, imprisoned, starved, chased, terrified out of your life, insulted, jeered at, and ignominiously flung into the water—by a woman, too! Where's the amusement in that? Where does the fun come in? And all because you must needs go and steal a motor-car. You know that you've never had anything but trouble from motor-cars from the moment you first set eyes on one. But if you *will* be mixed up with them—as you generally are, five minutes after you've started—why *steal* them? Be a cripple, if you think it's exciting; be a bankrupt, for a change, if you've set your mind on it; but why choose to be a convict? When are you going to be sensible, and think of your friends, and try and be a credit to them? Do you suppose it's any pleasure for me, for instance, to hear animals saying, as I go about, that I'm the chap that keeps company with gaol-birds?

"Young Goodman Brown" by Nathaniel Hawthorne

Short story
F/M, 20+
Salem, Massachusetts, circa 1690
Dramatic

Led by a spirit, Young Goodman Brown discovers evil at the heart of human nature.

• • •

Welcome, my children, (said the dark figure) to the communion of your race! Ye have found, thus young, your nature and your destiny. My children, look behind you! (...)

There (...) are all whom ye have reverenced from youth. Ye deemed them holier than yourselves, and shrank from your own sin, contrasting it with their lives of righteousness and prayerful aspirations heavenward. Yet, here are they all, in my worshipping assembly! This night it shall be granted you to know their secret deeds; how hoary-bearded elders of the church have whispered wanton words to the young maids of their households; how many a woman, eager for widow's weeds, has given her husband a drink at bedtime, and let him sleep his last sleep in her bosom; how beardless youths have made haste to inherit their father's wealth; and how fair damsels—blush not, sweet ones!—have dug little graves in the garden, and bidden me, the sole guest, to an infant's funeral. By the sympathy of your human hearts for sin, ye shall scent out all the places—whether in church, bed-chamber, street, field, or forest—where crime has been committed, and shall exult to behold the whole earth one stain of guilt, one mighty blood-spot.

Far more than this! It shall be yours to penetrate, in every bosom, the deep mystery of sin, the fountain of all wicked arts, and which inexhaustibly supplies more evil impulses than human power—than my power, at its utmost!—can make manifest in deeds. And now, my children, look upon each other.

INDEX OF MONOLOGUES
WITH SPECIAL VOICE CONSIDERATIONS

INDEX OF MONOLOGUES BY AUTHOR

256 indices

indices 257

INDEX BY SEX AND AGE

MALE MONOLOGUES BY AGE

INDEX OF MONOLOGUES BY TONE

SERIOCOMIC MONOLOGUES

PERMISSIONS

Every effort has been made to locate the proper copyright holder for each excerpt published in this anthology. Any discrepancies or exclusions are unintentional.

CAUTION: Professionals and amateurs are hereby warned that performance of each excerpt is subject to royalty. It is fully protected under the copy right laws of the United States of America and of all countries covered by the International Copyright Union (including the Dominion of Canada and the rest of the British Commonwealth), and all by the Pan-American Copyright Convention and the Universal Copyright Convention, the Berne Convention and of all countries with which the United States copyright relations. All rights, including professional, amateur/motion picture stage rights, recitation, lecturing, public reading, radio broadcasting, television, video or sound recording, all other forms of mechanical or electronic reproduction, such as CD-ROM, CD-1, information storage and retrieval systems and photocopying, and the rights of translation into foreign languages are strictly reserved. Particular emphasis is laid upon the matter of reading, permission for which must be obtained from the author's agent in writing.

8-BALL CHICKS: A YEAR IN THE VIOLENT WORLD OF GIRL by Gini Sikes. Copyright ©1997 by Gini Sikes. Reprinted by permission of Doubleday, a division of Random House. All inquiries should be sent to: The Doubleday Broadway Publishing Group, 1540 Broadway, New York, NY 10036.

"ADIRONDACK IRON" from RULE OF THE BONE by Russell Banks. Copyright ©1995 by Russell Banks. Reprinted by permission of HarperCollins Publishers, Inc. All inquiries should be sent to: HarperCollins Publishers, 10 East 53rd Street, New York, NY 10022-5299.

AFFLICTION by Russell Banks. Copyright ©1989 by Russell Banks. Reprinted by permission of HarperCollins Publisher, Inc. All inquiries should be directed to: HarperCollins Publishers, 10 East 53rd Street, New York, NY 10022-5299.

THE AGE OF GRIEF by Jane Smiley. Copyright ©1987 by Jane Smiley. Reprinted by permission of Alfred A. Knopf, a division of Random House, Inc. All inquiries should be sent to: Random House, Inc., Permissions Department, 299 Park Avenue, New York, NY 10171, Attn: Michael Greaves.

"AN ANGEL" from GOOD BONES AND SIMPLE MURDERS by Margaret Atwood. Copyright ©1983, 1992, 1994 by O.W. Toad Ltd. A Nan A. Talese Book. Reprinted by permission of Doubleday,a division of Random House. All inquiries should be sent to: The Doubleday Broadway Publishing Group, 1540 Broadway, New York, NY 10036.

ENDURING LOVE by Ian McEwan. Copyright ©1997 by Ian McEwan. Reprinted by permission of Doubleday, a division of Random House, Inc. All inquiries should be sent to: The Doubleday Broadway Publishing Group, 1540 Broadway, New York, NY 10036.

"ETIOLOGY" from GIRL, INTERRUPTED by Susanna Kaysen. Copyright ©1993 by Susanna Kaysen. Reprinted by permission of Random House, Inc. All inquiries should be sent to: Random House, Inc., Permissions Department, 299 Park Avenue, New York, NY 10171, Attn: Diana Harrington.

"EVERYTHING IS GREEN" from THE GIRL WITH CURIOUS HAIR by David Foster Wallace. Copyright ©1989 by David Foster Wallace. Reprinted by permission of W.W. Norton & Company, Inc. All inquiries should be sent to: W.W. Norton & Company, 500 Fifth Avenue, New York, NY 10110-0017.

THE FIRST DANCE by Irene Zahava. Copyright ©1990 by Irene Zahava. Reprinted by permission of the Author. All inquiries should be sent to: Irene Zahava, 307 West State, Ithaca, NY 14850, zee@twcny.rr.com.

FISHBOY by Mark Richard. Copyright ©1993 by Mark Richard. Reprinted by permission of Doubleday, a division of Random House, Inc. All inquiries should be sent to: The Doubleday Broadway Publishing Group, 1540 Broadway, New York, NY 10036.

FOR JEROMÉ – WITH LOVE AND KISSES by Gordon Lish. Copyright ©1983, 1984, 1986 and 1996 by Gordon Lish. Reprinted by permission of the Author. All inquiries should be sent to: Gordon Lish, 8 East 96th Street, New York, NY 10128.

FREEDOMLAND by Richard Price. Copyright ©1998 by Richard Price. Reprinted by permission of Broadway Books, a division of Random House. All inquiries should be sent to: The Doubleday Broadway Publishing Group, 1540 Broadway, New York, NY 10036.

FRIED GREEN TOMATOES AT THE WHISTLE STOP CAFÉ by Fannie Flagg. Copyright ©1987 by Fannie Flagg. Reprinted by permission of Random House, Inc. All inquiries should be sent to: Random House, Inc., Permissions Department, 299 Park Avenue, New York, NY 10171.

GEEK LOVE by Katherine Dunn. Copyright ©1989 by Katherine Dunn. Reprinted by permission of Alfred A. Knopf, a division of Random House, Inc. All inquiries should be sent to: Random House, Inc., Permissions Department, 299 Park Avenue, New York, NY 10171, Attn: Michael Greaves.

GERTRUDE AND CLAUDIUS by John Updike. Copyright ©2000 by John Updike. Reprinted by permission of Alfred A. Knopf, a division of Random House, Inc. All inquiries should be sent to:

Random House, Inc., Permissions Department, 299 Park Avenue, New York, NY 10171, Attn: Michael Greaves.

"GERTRUDE TALKS BACK" from GOOD BONES AND SIMPLE MURDERS by Margaret Atwood. Copyright ©1983, 1992, 1994 by O.W. Toad Ltd. A Nan A. Talese Book. Reprinted by permission of Doubleday,a division of Random House. All inquiries should be sent to: The Doubleday Broadway Publishing Group, 1540 Broadway, New York, NY 10036.

THE GIANT'S HOUSE by Elizabeth McCracken. Copyright ©1996 by Elizabeth McCracken. Reprinted by permission of Dell Publishing, a division of Random House, Inc. All inquiries should be sent to: Dell Publishing, 1540 Broadway, New York, NY 10036.

GLORY GOES AND GETS SOME by Emily Carter. Copyright ©1998 by Emily Carter. Reprinted by permission of International Creative Management. All inquiries should be sent to: 40 West 57th Street, New York, NY 10019.

"UNTITLED" from GREEK LYRICS by Theognis, translated by Richard Lattimore. Copyright ©1960 by Richard Lattimore. Reprinted by permission of University of Chicago Press. All inquiries should be sent to: The University of Chicago Press, Permissions Department, 5801 South Ellis Avenue, Chicago, IL 60637.

HALF A LIFE by Jill Ciment. Copyright ©1996 by Jill Ciment. Reprinted by permission of Crown Publishers, a division of Random House, Inc. All inquiries should be sent to: Random House, Inc., Permissions Department, 299 Park Avenue, New York, NY 10171, Attn: Elizabeth Herr.

"HALFWAY HOME" by Paul Monette. Copyright ©1991 by Paul Monette. Reprinted by permission of Crown Publishers, a division of Random House, Inc. All inquiries should be sent to: Random House, Inc., Permissions Department, 299 Park Avenue, New York, NY 10171.

"HARD SELL" from IF THE RIVER WAS WHISKEY by T. Coraghessan Boyle. Copyright ©1989 by T. Coraghessan Boyle. Reprinted by permission of Viking Penguin, a division of Penguin Putnam Inc. All inquiries should be sent to: Penguin Putnam Inc., 375 Hudson Street, New York, NY 10014.

HELP ME FIND MY SPACEMAN LOVER from TABLOID DREAMS by Robert Olen Butler. Copyright ©1996 by Robert Olen Butler. Reprinted by permission of Henry Holt and Company, LLC. All inquiries should be sent to: Henry Holt and Company, LLC, 115 West 18th Street, New York, NY 10011.

Irene Ziegler is an actor, teacher, playwright, and novelist. Most recently, she played Maggie Runyon in *The Contender* (nominated for two Academy Awards) and can currently be seen as Mrs. Laughlin in the series, *Going To California.* She has taught speech, oral interpretation, or acting at Eastern Michigan University, Old Dominion University, and the University of Richmond, where she was an Artist in Residence. Her collection of linked short stories, *Rules of the Lake,* was chosen as a Best Book for Young Adults by the New York City Public Library, and the one-woman play of the same name won the Mary Roberts Rinehart Award. She is currently at work on a thriller. She has a ten-year-old son. They in live in Richmond, Virginia.

Laurie Walker has taught English literature, writing, reading, art, and college success since 1982 for the Ypsilanti and Ann Arbor Public Schools, The University of Michigan and Eastern Michigan University. Currently teaching literature, writing and freshmen seminar courses at EMU, she is co-author, with Robert Holkeboer, of *Right from The Start: Taking Charge of Your College Success.* Laurie also recently wrote the collaborative learning and peer editing strand of *The Bedford Guide for College Writers, 6/e.* Laurie has extensive freelance editing and graphic art experience, two grown daughters, one registered domestic partner, two cats, and one boa constrictor. She lives and works in Ypsilanti, Michigan.

John Capecci holds a Ph.D. in Speech Communication and has nearly twenty years experience coaching, teaching, and presenting public performances. Formerly a graduate instructor at the University of North Carolina-Chapel Hill and professor at Eastern Michigan University, John has taught communication techniques and performance theory and practice to high school, undergraduate, graduate, and adult learners, and he has published essays on the performance of literature. In 1999, he founded Ecco Communications, a national network of communication trainers and educators, based in Minneapolis.